CASHLESS

MARK HITCHCOCK

HARVEST HOUSE PUBLISHERS

EUGENE, OREGON

Cover by Abris, Veneta, Oregon

Published in association with William K. Jensen Literary Agency, 119 Bampton Court, Eugene, Oregon 97404.

CASHLESS
Copyright © 2009 by Mark Hitchcock
Published by Harvest House Publishers
Eugene, Oregon 97402
www.harvesthousepublishers.com

Library of Congress Cataloging-in-Publication Data
  Hitchcock, Mark.
  Cashless / Mark Hitchcock.
    p. cm.
  Includes bibliographical references.
  ISBN 978-0-7369-2644-7 (pbk.)
  1. Economics—Religious aspects—Christianity. 2. Economics in the Bible. 3. Bible—Prophecies—Armageddon. 4. Finance, Personal—Biblical teaching 5. Armageddon—Biblical teaching. I. Title.
  BR115.E3H58 2009
  236'.9—dc22
                              2009011523

Printed in the United States of America

09 10 11 12 13 14 15 16 17 / DP-NI / 10 9 8 7 6 5 4 3 2 1

CONTENTS

To Justin
You are a wise son who brings
untold blessing and joy to my life.
I'm proud to be your father.

Chips can be programmed to store monetary value, just like EZ-Pass and Metrocard. If such a chip were implanted in the fleshy part of the palm of the hand, with a wave we could pay highway tolls, pass through subway and bus turnstiles and breeze through the supermarket checkout. Just think of the value to society: no more cash to worry about, or waiting for change, and no more muggings. This is the cashless society we have been dreaming of for years.

JEFFREY O. MILMAN
The New York Times (June 24, 1999)

FINANCIAL APOCALYPSE BRINGS AN ECONOMIC NEW WORLD ORDER

The Nightmare on Wall Street Sets the Stage

"2009 will mark the beginning of a new world order."

HENRY KISSINGER
(November 2008)

"Once the smoke clears, I suspect we will find ourselves living in a world of globalization on steroids—a world in which key global economies are more intimately tied together than ever before."

THOMAS FRIEDMAN
The New York Times
(October 19, 2008)

"There is a global meltdown coming...And one world currency and one world financial system is the endgame...China said last week they want one global currency. France said yesterday they want one world order—a new world order at the end of this event."

GLENN BECK
(October 9, 2008)

The headlines stunned us all:

"Bailout Nation," *Time* (September 22, 2008)

"Wall Street Financial Meltdown," *USA Today* (September 30, 2008)

"Wall Street Panics; markets lose $1 trillion: Dow plunges 778 points," *Washington Times* (September 30, 2008)

"The Fall of America, Inc.," *Newsweek* (October 4, 2008)

"America's Credit Catastrophe," *U.S. News & World Report* (October 3, 2008)

"The New Hard Times," *Time* (October 13, 2008)

"How Scared Should You Be," *U.S. News & World Report* (October 3, 2008)

The long-predicted financial meltdown of America's debt-ridden economy finally arrived in the fall of 2008. The elements of an economic "perfect storm" converged. The chickens of our casino culture came home to roost. The nightmare on Wall Street finally hit.

Day after day, a cascade of bad news continued to gush forth. We witnessed the near-collapse of the entire investment banking sector and the fall of insurance giant AIG. Fannie Mae and Freddie Mac imploded. Carnage on Wall Street ensued. World markets plunged. For sure, the United States experienced the most serious economic earthquake since the Great Depression, and some even believe these seismic events were on the scale of the 1929 crash. I've heard it described as "Fiscal Armageddon." The fallout was dramatic as we entered uncharted economic waters. All the old financial paradigms were thrown out the window. Even the experts were at a loss over what to do. The aftershocks reverberated through every area of the economy. America as we know it was changed forever. This was the equivalent of an "economic 9/11" for America and the world. The word of the year in 2008, according to Merriam-Webster, was *bailout*. Webster's definition for this word is "a rescue from financial distress." The oft-repeated joke was that everyone's 401(k) had suddenly become a 201(k). Yet we all knew this was no laughing matter.

One *Newsweek* headline summed up what many were thinking: "The Quitter Economy: Companies are liquidating; homeowners are mailing in the keys. Have we given up?" (February 2, 2009). In January 2009 alone, 600,000 jobs were lost making the downturn the worst for unemployment in the post-WWII era.[1] Then in just one week in February 2009, another 600,000 jobs were lost. Unemployment approached 10 percent. America and the world faced the possibility of a devastating downward economic spiral. Spending and confidence tumbled worldwide. The crisis was dubbed the Great Recession. In the fourth quarter of 2008 the U.S. economy contracted at almost 4 percent annual rate. In Japan (fall of 13 percent) and Europe (6 percent decline) it was even worse.[2] Everyone was asking the same questions: How could this happen? What does it all mean? Where are we headed?

But there's another question lurking in the background that many people may have never considered. What if the global financial chaos is not just a massive economic meltdown but the genesis of a dramatic, tectonic shift toward a global economic system? A system that will ultimately be controlled by one man. A system that will ultimately require all people to be registered and submit to him. What if it's the first domino to fall in a chain of events that is setting the stage for the economy of the end times? Such a new world order was foretold by the biblical prophets long ago.

Think Globally

The financial tsunami hit with brutal force and caught many by surprise. Many questions remain unanswered, but one fact became immediately clear: We live in a global economy. Megatrends affect the whole globe simultaneously. In the Internet age, the new economy is more deeply interconnected than ever. It is built on global trade, global capital markets, and global communication. National economies respond to the same forces and rise and fall together. Markets around the world responded immediately to the massive credit crunch in the United States. Precipitous declines struck the markets in Europe, Japan, Russia, and Hong Kong.

As the markets descended into chaos, the governments of the world swung into action to stave off a global financial collapse. This immediately paved the way for greater international cooperation and oversight of the world economy. The nations of the world scrambled for solutions. President Bush visited the headquarters of the 185-nation International Monetary Fund (IMF) and met with G-7 leaders. Treasury Secretary Henry Paulson and Federal Reserve Chairman Ben Bernanke participated in discussions with the "Group of 20" or G-20, which is an international organization that includes the leaders of 19 of the world's biggest national economies, plus the entire European Union (EU). The EU came together in a show of force and unity with proposed solutions to the increasingly shaky global economy. Key nations acted in unparalleled unison to drop interest rates to squeeze some liquidity into world financial markets. There were heightened calls for some kind of international oversight of the world's banking and financial institutions. Many believe there is a need to create an international financial system that is governed by global regulations and overseen by a global regulator.

The global cooperation was astonishing, but should not be surprising. In times of financial turmoil, people are willing to surrender freedoms, make concessions, and cooperate in ways that they wouldn't in calmer times. People in pain are willing to go along with almost anything the government proposes if it can stop the economic bleeding. Several years ago, I read that in the Chinese language the word *crisis is* made up of two characters signifying "opportunity" and "danger." Not knowing Chinese, I have to take the person's word that this is true. But whether this piece of linguistic trivia is accurate or not, we all know from experience that it's true that a time of great crisis, while carrying the potential for danger, opens up opportunities for those who are ready to seize them. Every crisis affords opportunity to those who will step forward, whether it be a personal or family crisis, or a global crisis.

White House Chief of Staff Rahm Emanuel, in November 2008, expressed this sentiment in a statement he made about the economic crisis: "You never want a serious crisis to go to waste. This crisis provides the opportunity for us to do things that you could not do before." Emanuel probably wished later that he hadn't said that, but it certainly expressed what he believes. And the principle he stated, though usually unspoken, is recognized by every leader: Crisis equals opportunity. The world has witnessed this again and again. For example, during the 1930s in America, Franklin Roosevelt was given wide latitude and backing to enact almost any legislation he wanted. And in Germany, a downward economic spiral allowed a madman like Adolf Hitler to draw tens of thousand to his rallies by promising to restore prosperity. A few years later he assumed power and swayed the German people to follow his insanity for over ten years.

Government Takeover

Going into 2009, unemployment in the United States skyrocketed to levels not seen in decades. Recession teetered perilously on the precipice of depression. America's national debt now stands at a staggering $11 trillion dollars—and counting. The numbers on America's infamous debt clock near New York's Times Square have been spinning like the dial on Clark Griswold's electric meter. And added to the $11 trillion is another $53 trillion of unfunded public promises in the form of Social Security and Medicare. That's $175,000 for every American—and rising. Given the current trends, this will amount to about 240 percent of GDP (Gross Domestic Product) by 2040, up from an almost manageable 65 percent today.[3] David Walker tried to get the nation's attention in 2008 when he released the aptly titled movie *I.O.U.S.A.*

To solve America's economic mess, the government has taken on a growing role in the economy. The economic stimulus bill signed in February 2009, the largest spending bill in U.S. history, carried a staggering $789 billion price tag. Massive government spending and increasing control are leading many to point out that the United States is looking increasing like a modern European state.[4] The size of the U.S. government will increase to 40 percent of the U.S. economy by 2010.[5]

Major financial institutions have been nationalized, leading many to note that America is on the road to socialism. *Newsweek*'s attention-grabbing cover story on February 16, 2009, was

"We Are All Socialists Now." That same issue of *Newsweek* ran an article titled "Big Government is Back—Big Time," which highlights the fact that more and more Americans are looking to the government for support. Cradle-to-grave entitlements have led to dubbing America to be a "nanny state." There's no doubt that on every front, economic power is becoming more and more centralized both domestically and internationally. The words of Thomas Jefferson are a stark reminder and warning: "A government big enough to give you everything you want is strong enough to take everything you have." And according to the Bible, that's exactly where all of this is ultimately headed.

The New World Order

The economic Armageddon the world has experienced could be the initial explosion that sets in motion a chain reaction of events that eventually lead to the global system foretold by the prophets of old. Globalists have seized the opportunity created by the 2008 financial tsunami and the ensuing spirit of cooperation to further entwine world economies and step up moves for a more centralized authority and oversight. And the prediction of a financial new world order was front-page news:

> "There is going to be a new financial world order that will be born of this" (*Bloomberg,* September 16, 2008)
>
> "Financial Crisis Reshapes World Order" (*Washington Post,* October 12, 2008)
>
> "G-7 Sets Sights on New World Order" (Agence France-Presse, February 15, 2009)

The emergency worldwide economic summit of the G-20 nations in Washington in November 2008 was a kind of first step toward further cementing the world together economically. The call for a global economy was heard round the world. Britain's prime minister, Gordon Brown, immediately jumped on the global bandwagon. He viewed the 2008 financial crash that engulfed the world as a unique opportunity:

> And if we learn from our experience of turning unity of purpose into unity of action, we can together seize this moment of change in our world to create a truly global society...My message is that we must be: internationalist not protectionist; interventionist not neutral; progressive not reactive; and forward-looking not frozen by events. We can seize the moment and in doing so build a truly global society.[6]

In March 2009, in preparation for another meeting of the G-20, Brown's rhetoric soared even higher when he began to promote what he called a "global new deal." He met with President Obama of the United States to discuss what he referred to as "a global new deal, whose impact can stretch from the villages of Africa to reforming the financial institutions of London and New York—and giving security to the hard-working families in every country." He continued: "It is a global new deal that will lay the foundations not just for a sustainable economic recovery but for a genuinely new era of international partnership in which all countries have a part to play."[7] Brown also said, "We need a global New Deal—a grand bargain between the countries and continents of this world—so that the world economy can not only recover but...so the banking system can be based on...best principles." Brown believes that this could happen quickly. He said, "There is the possibility in the next few months of a global new deal that will involve all the countries of the world in sorting out and cleaning up the banking system." German chancellor Angela Merkel supports Brown's bold new initiative. She proposed that a new institution grow out of the crisis—one that "will take on more responsibility for global [financial] mechanisms."[7]

The *Los Angeles Times* also pointed toward a new global strategy as the answer:

> The way the current financial crisis spread around the world like a brush fire, outracing all efforts to contain it, underscored a painful reality: We have a global economy but nothing close to a global system for managing it. The world may be flat when it comes to the increasingly interconnected economies of the 21st century, but it still has borders—and conflicting national interests to go with them...the question is whether the worst economic crisis since before World War II will open the door for a comprehensive, unified economic strategy.[8]

People everywhere are calling for a global fix. The world faces the biggest reshaping of the financial system since the Great Depression. National economies are being transformed into a global one. Robert Reich, the former labor secretary under President Clinton, sees globalism as an inescapable economic force. "We are living through a transformation that will rearrange the politics and economics of the coming century...Each nation's primary political task will be to cope with the centrifugal forces of the global economy."[9] Alex Patelis, head of international economics at Merrill Lynch, said, "We do need a new world financial order, and we will probably get one as a side effect of this crisis."[10] Peter Kenny, managing director of Knight Capital Group, said,

"The tectonic plates beneath the world financial system are shifting, and there is going to be a new financial world order that will be born of this."[11]

There have even been increased calls for a global economic "policeman" that will serve as a kind of United Nations for the world economy. *The Telegraph* reports:

> So, as the world's central bankers gather this week in Washington DC for an IMF-World Bank conference to discuss the crisis, the big question they face is whether it is time to establish a global economic "policeman" to ensure the crash of 2008 can never be repeated... In essence, any organization with the power to police the global economy would have to include representatives of every major country—a United Nations of economic regulation.[12]

All of a sudden the phrase *new world order* is on the lips of financial policy gurus. "The phrase 'new world order' traces back at least as far as 1940, when author H.G. Wells used it as the title of a book about a socialist, unified, one-world government. The phrase has also been linked to American presidents, including Woodrow Wilson, whose work on establishing the League of Nations pioneered the concept of international government bodies, and to the first President Bush, who used it in a 1989 speech."[13] Speaking at the Business Council for the United Nations on September 14, 1994, David Rockefeller looked forward to some great crisis that could spark the new world order: "We are on the verge of a global transformation. All we need is the right major crisis and the nations will accept the New World Order."[14] The current economic meltdown is the major crisis the globalists have been looking for.

One of the chief proponents and strategists for the new world order is former Secretary of State Henry Kissinger, a member of the Council on Foreign Relations. In January 2009, Kissinger said this:

> There is a need for a new world order. I think that at the end of this administration, with all its turmoil, and at the beginning of the next, we might actually witness the creation of a new order—because people looking in the abyss...have to conclude that at some point, ordered expectations must return under a different system...The president-elect is coming into office at a moment when there is upheaval in many parts of the world simultaneously...You have India, Pakistan; you have the jihadist movement. So he can't really say there is one problem, that it's the most important one. But he can give new impetus to American foreign policy partly because the reception of him is so extraordinary around the world. His task will be to develop an overall strategy for America in this period when, really, a new world order can be created. It's a great opportunity, it isn't just a crisis... Within the next four years we will witness the emergence of a "New International Order."[15]

Kissinger continued:

> In the end, the political and economic systems can be harmonized in only one of two ways: by creating an international political regulatory system with the same reach as that of the economic world...or by shrinking the economic units to a size manageable by existing political structures, which is likely to lead to a new mercantilism, perhaps of regional units.[16]

Kissinger clearly favors the more global approach. He continued laying out his global vision: "The economic world has been globalized…[the] world financial mess is not a crisis, but an opportunity to forge a New World Order, politically, but primarily economic."[17] Make no mistake—Kissinger and other globalists intend to take full advantage of the world financial meltdown to justify and advance their vision and forge a global economy.

Klaus Schwab is the founder of the World Economic Forum in Davos, Switzerland. When the forum met in January 2009, the 2000 business and political leaders in attendance described the world economic disaster as a "crisis of capitalism." The official theme of the 2009 forum was "shaping the post-crisis world." Klaus Schwab referred to the global economic meltdown as a "transformational crisis." He urged the delegates to respond to the crisis by shaping a "new world order." Schwab said: "Above all else this is a crisis of confidence. To restore confidence you have to establish signposts that the world after the crisis will be different. We have to create a new world."[18] He also announced the need for a "global redesign initiative" to rebuild the global economic system.

The G-20 leaders met again in London on April 2, 2009 amidst calls for a new "Bretton Woods" financial framework. Bretton Woods is a mountain resort in New Hampshire where 44 Allied nations met in 1944 to hammer out a plan for the postwar financial system. Bretton Woods is where the International Monetary Fund (IMF) and the World Bank were conceived, as well as the "fixed exchange rates built around the U.S. dollar that was linked to gold."[19] That was the first tangible step toward a global economy. A new Bretton Woods would be a huge second step.

The current financial mess has exponentially accelerated calls for an entirely new global financial infrastructure. Nations such as China, Germany, and Brazil believe that big changes are needed. A growing choir of international voices is calling for global laws and regulations, including a much stronger IMF that will function as a central bank to the world. China and Russia have urged the world to create a new global currency to replace the U.S. dollar.[20] All of these efforts are aimed at solidifying the world economically. The independent financial sovereignty of nations is rapidly becoming a thing of the past.

Already the G-7, an exclusive club of wealthy nations, has called for the creation of a "college of supervisors" to more closely oversee and coordinate the regulation of multinational banks. The Group of Thirty, an influential organization of former and current central bankers and financial regulators, is recommending that large financial institutions be subjected to tougher requirements and regulations. Clearly, change is on the way, and the change that's coming is sweeping. Unstoppable forces have been unleashed that will change the world forever.

Drastic, transformational changes in attitudes usually come about when there is a crisis grave enough to justify the shift. As the old saying goes, "Desperate times call for desperate measures." The current world financial chaos may be the catalyst that ushers in the new world order that globalists have dreamed about for so long.

Why Globalism?

It might be helpful at this point to pause for a moment and briefly consider why so many powerful political and economic insiders want a global economy. What's so great about globalism? While globalists can probably give many reasons in support of their goals, two stand out from the rest. First, they say it is far more economically advantageous to have the entire world as your market rather than one nation or even a region. They see simple mass marketing on a greater scale as beneficial. Second, globalists believe that the more the nations of the world are economically intertwined, the less likely it is that they will start wars against one another. Both of these justifications are true, but the danger of globalism is that it will "grease the skids" for the coming of the slickest politician the world has ever known, the Antichrist, who will one day seize the reins of world power and the global economy to advance his own agenda.[21]

Crucial Technology Is Here

The current worldwide economic chaos is clearly a driving force in bringing the countries of the world together in an unprecedented way. But it's not the only force. Over the last 20 years, we have witnessed an exponential leap in the technology that is necessary for the end-time global system to be put in place. The staggering advances made with computers, related electronic technologies, and biometrics is drawing the nations of the world closer and closer to total interdependence and globalization. This technology is related to every area of modern life: banking, commerce, communications, and transportation. Financial catastrophe, "transformational crisis," and mind-boggling technology are converging to usher in a financial new world order.

Signs of the Times

Economic globalization and the technology to support it could be one of the most important signs of the times. Amazingly, the

Bible predicted over 1900 years ago that one man, the coming Antichrist, will ultimately take control of the entire world's economy. Many have wondered how this could ever happen. What could possibly transpire to bring the economies of the world under the umbrella of a central authority? We may now have the answer. The prerequisites to make this prophecy possible are here.

The biblical entry point for any discussion of the one-world economic system, a cashless society, and end-time prophecy is Revelation 13:16-18:

> He causes all, the small and the great, and the rich and the poor, and the free men and the slaves, to be given a mark on their right hand or on their forehead, and he provides that no one should be able to buy or to sell, except the one who has the mark, either the name of the beast or the number of his name. Here is wisdom. Let him who has understanding calculate the number of the beast, for the number is that of a man; and his number is six hundred and sixty-six.

The Bible clearly links the global mark of the beast system with the emergence of a cashless society. We will discuss all this more in later chapters. But it seems clear to many people that what we see today is a frightening foreshadow and portent of what's coming. While no one on earth knows what the final fallout will be from the world economic crisis, it's clear that the world is ripe for a universal economic strategy and a charismatic leader to bring the world together. As prophecy teacher Phillip Goodman notes, "The political winds of our time are full speed ahead to take America's economy—and that of all nations—and force-fit them into a global economic framework which will provide yet another sign that the world stage is being set for the arrival of the ultimate political, military, religious and economic czar, the Antichrist."[22]

FAQ (Frequently Asked Questions)

Looking beyond financial meltdown and chaos to where it's all headed, here are some of the questions this book will seek to answer:

Will there be a one-world economy in the end times?

What will it look like?

Does the Bible predict a cashless society?

How is the stage being set for a cashless society?

What is the mark of the beast?

What's the significance of the number 666?

What's the purpose of the mark?

Does modern technology relate to the mark of the beast?

We will explore these questions and many more in the pages that follow. To answer these questions we must consult two main sources—the Bible and current events. Any relevant discussion of the coming cashless society must consider today's news and current advances in technology, and be moored in the major prophetic declarations found in Scripture. As one preacher is quoted to have said, "We need to have a copy of the Bible in one hand and the newspaper in the other."

It now appears that it's no longer a matter of *if* but *when* a one-world global economy emerges, and that it will be some form of a cashless system. It also appears that current economic and technological trends and developments are hurriedly setting the stage for the final chapter of this age as described in the Bible. The mechanism for controlling all commerce by controlling economic transactions and banking could not have been imagined in the past.

But not anymore.

2

THE FUTURE HAS ALREADY BEEN WRITTEN

How Close Are We to the Final Act?

> *"We should all be concerned about the future because we will have to spend the rest of our lives there."*
>
> CHARLES F. KETTERING

> *"The trouble with our times is that the future is not what it used to be."*
>
> PAUL VALERY

Sometimes in life we feel like we have entered a dark theater near the end of a play with several acts. We didn't write the play. We didn't ask to be thrust into it. We can be certain this drama is near the last act. Even though we did not see the beginning, we can look back and see the plot and direction of the play. But even then, how can we be sure when the next act will start?

When it comes to world history, the biblical prophets talked a lot about the last act. To determine whether it is drawing near, we need to look for the events that set up the last act. If those events are occurring now, we can be fairly certain the last act is just ahead. What are the events, the characters, and the plot that will bring the play of world history to its predicted climax? Will we be wise enough to see it coming? Will we be ready?

The only way we can be ready is if we know something about the last act. God has not told us everything about the final drama, but He has given us some insights into the plot, main characters, key events, and the ending of the story. Bible prophecy is the lens through which we can gain a better sense of the significance of today's headlines.

Reviewing the Final Act

Before we get into the specific details of the coming one-world economy and cashless society and what the Bible says about it, let's gather all the information we can about the last act in world history, because even before the final act plays out, a number of preliminary moves, which are predicted in the Bible, will shape the political, economic, and religious climate necessary for the end times to arrive. These preliminary moves are now falling into place in rapid succession. As these moves are completed, a more specific timetable of events can begin.

The Bible provides a basic outline of the major stages or phases of the final act. To help us get our biblical bearings, let's look at ten key end-time markers on the road to Armageddon—markers that will help us get a handle on where things are headed. These markers are prophetic signposts that could help us see how close the final act may be.

Ten Key End-Time Markers

1. A Stunning Disappearance

The world will be traumatized by the fulfillment of what theologians call the rapture of the church—the sudden removal of every Christian from the world. The rapture, the next great event on God's prophetic calendar, is vividly described in 1 Thessalonians 4:13-18:

> We do not want you to be uninformed, brethren, about those who are asleep, so that you will not grieve as do the rest who have no hope. For if we believe that Jesus died and rose again, even so God will bring with Him those who have fallen asleep in Jesus. For this we say to you by the word of the Lord, that we who are alive and remain until the coming of the Lord, will not precede those who have fallen asleep. For the Lord Himself will descend from heaven with a shout, with the voice of the archangel and with the trumpet of God, and the dead in Christ will rise first. Then we who are alive and remain will be caught up together with them in the clouds to meet the Lord in the air, and so we shall always be with the Lord. Therefore comfort one another with these words.

The rapture is also described by the apostle Paul in 1 Corinthians 15:50-53:

> Now I say this, brethren, that flesh and blood cannot inherit the kingdom of God; nor does the perishable inherit the imperishable. Behold, I tell you a mystery; we will not all sleep, but we will all be changed, in a moment, in the twinkling of an eye, at the last trumpet; for the trumpet will sound, and the dead will be

raised imperishable, and we will be changed. For this perishable must put on the imperishable, and this mortal must put on immortality.

The rapture will fulfill the promise Jesus gave to His disciples in John 14:3: "I will come again, and receive you to Myself, that where I am, there you may be also." At that time, all true Christians who have died will be resurrected, and every true Christian who is still alive on earth will be taken up into heaven without experiencing death. As you can imagine, the sudden disappearance of millions of Christians worldwide will deepen the religious confusion already widespread in today's culture. The organized church, with every true Christian removed, will fall into the hands of self-seeking opportunists. An event as dramatic as the rapture will also undoubtedly have economic repercussions that could move the nations further down the road to a one-world economic system.

2. A Season of Further Preparation

Immediately after the rapture will come a period of further preparation for the end times. It's important to remember that the rapture itself doesn't begin the seven-year Tribulation. Days, weeks, months, or even years could go by between the rapture and the beginning of the Tribulation—however, a period of a few months makes the most sense to me. As you can imagine, after the great confusion created by the rapture, some amount of time will have to pass for life on earth to return to any semblance of normalcy. During this time of expanded stage setting, many events will occur that are necessary to further lay the groundwork for the end times.

3. The Rise of the G-10

One of the central developments during this time of preparation is the rise of a group of ten world leaders who will emerge on the world stage and consolidate the power of the West. Today, we often hear about the G-7, G-20, and G-30. These are various groups of nations that have joined together in economic cooperation to work toward common goals. We could call this particular end-time group of leaders the G-10 or Group of Ten. This ruling group, committee, or oligarchy will unite the European and Mediterranean countries into a new revived and powerful Western coalition like the ancient Roman Empire. The G-10 is represented by the ten toes on the image in King Nebuchadnezzar's dream in Daniel 2:41-44, and the ten horns on the wild beast in Daniel 7:7,24.

The G-10 may well be the iron fist that the world looks to for help in stopping the chaos after the rapture. What we see today in the European Union could be the initial stages of this coming political, economic union that will coalesce under the rule of ten leaders.

4. Antichrist Rising

At the conclusion of this period of preparation after the rapture, a powerful ruler will arise (Daniel 9:26) who will be elected as the head of the G-10 (Revelation 17:12-13). This "little horn" of Daniel 7:8 will begin in obscurity but will quickly ascend to take over the power consolidated by the G-10. A political unknown, he will come out of nowhere to rise to supremacy. Taking full advantage of his awe-inspiring charisma and mesmerizing speaking ability, he will take the world political scene by storm.

5. The New Pax Romana

This brilliant leader will launch his career by doing something that no world leader up to now has been able to do. He will convince or possibly even compel the state of Israel and evidently its worst enemies to enter into some kind of peace treaty. The length of the treaty will be seven years (Daniel 9:27). The signing of this covenant marks the beginning of what is commonly described as the seven-year Tribulation period. This treaty will usher in an era of false peace, a move toward disarmament, and a major push for a new world economic system. The first three-and-a-half years of this seven-year period will be the calm before the storm as the new leader consolidates his power.

This mirrors what we see in today's headlines. People today are yearning for peace—almost desperately, and especially in the Middle East. The heralded Roadmap to Peace was laid out in 2003 by a powerful quartet: the United States, the European Union, the United Nations, and Russia. From the many negotiators and leaders involved in attempts to bring peace to the Middle East, one new international leader will eventually emerge from Europe to superimpose a peace settlement on Israel and her neighbors.

6. Terrible Tribulation

While the signing of this covenant will bring peace to the Middle East, at least for a brief period of time, it will also mark the beginning of the final seven years of this present age—a seven-year period of unparalleled turmoil and upheaval for the world. While many parts of the Bible give glimpses of this coming day of disaster, Revelation 6–19 is the main passage that describes this era. These fourteen chapters focus upon the terrible judgments God will send upon the earth during the end times. In these chapters we read of three sets of seven judgments that the

Lord will pour out on the world. There are seven seal judgments (Revelation 6), seven trumpet judgments (Revelation 8–9), and seven bowl judgments (Revelation 16). These series of judgments will be poured out successively during the Tribulation.

7 Seals ⟶ 7 Trumpets ⟶ 7 Bowls

I believe the seven seals will be opened during the first half of the tribulation. The seven trumpets will be blown during the second half of the Tribulation, and the seven bowls will be poured out in a very brief period of time right near the end of the Tribulation just before Christ returns.

First Half of Tribulation	Second Half of Tribulation	Second Coming
7 Seals	7 Trumpets	7 Bowls

In Scripture, these judgments are compared several times with birth pangs (Jeremiah 30:4-7; Matthew 24:8; 1 Thessalonians 5:3). As the Tribulation progresses, like birth pangs, these judgments will irreversibly intensify in their severity and frequency.

These three waves of God's judgment are described in detail in Revelation 6–19:

Seven Seal Judgments

First Seal (6:1-2)—White horse: Antichrist

Second Seal (6:3-4)—Red horse: war

Third Seal (6:5-6)—Black horse: famine

Fourth Seal (6:7-8)—Pale horse: death and hell

Fifth Seal (6:9-11)—Martyrs in heaven

Sixth Seal (6:12-17)—Universal upheaval and devastation

Seventh Seal (8:1-2)—The seven trumpets

Seven Trumpet Judgments

First Trumpet (8:7)—Bloody hail and fire: one-third of vegetation destroyed

Second Trumpet (8:8-9)—Fireball from heaven: one-third of oceans polluted

Third Trumpet (8:10-11)—Falling star: one-third of fresh water polluted

Fourth Trumpet (8:12)—Darkness: one-third of sun, moon, and stars darkened

Fifth Trumpet (9:1-12)—Demonic invasion: torment

Sixth Trumpet (9:13-21)—Demonic army: one-third of mankind killed

Seventh Trumpet (11:15-19)—The kingdom: the announcement of Christ's reign

Seven Bowl Judgments

First Bowl (16:2)—Upon the earth: sores on the worshippers of the Antichrist

Second Bowl (16:3)—Upon the seas: turned to blood

Third Bowl (16:4-7)—Upon the fresh water: turned to blood

Fourth Bowl (16:8-9)—Upon the sun: intense, scorching heat

Fifth Bowl (16:10-11)—Upon the Antichrist's kingdom: darkness and pain

Sixth Bowl (16:12-16)—Upon the River Euphrates: Armageddon

Seventh Bowl (16:17-21)—Upon the air: earthquakes and hail

It boggles the mind just to read this list. One-half of the earth's population will perish in just two of the 19 tribulation judgments.[1] In the fourth seal judgment, one-fourth of the world will die (Revelation 6:8); and in the fifth trumpet judgment, one-third will perish (Revelations 9:18).

The environment of the entire planet will be destroyed. Revelation 16:19-21 graphically pictures the worldwide devastation: "The cities of the nations fell…And every island fled away, and the mountains were not found. And huge hailstones, about one hundred pounds each, came down from heaven upon men."

Just think what it would be like to live on earth while all this is transpiring.

7. Israel's Pearl Harbor

Sometime during the first three-and-a-half years of the Tribulation, Russia and a group of Islamic allies will attempt a final bid for power in the Middle East. The prophet Ezekiel wrote about this 2600 years ago, yet his words read like today's headlines. Ezekiel listed the precise alliance of nations that will invade Israel in the latter years, or end times. The list is found in Ezekiel 38:1-6:

> The word of the LORD came to me saying, "Son of man, set your face toward Gog of the land of Magog, the prince of Rosh, Meshech and Tubal, and prophesy against him and say, 'Thus says the Lord GOD, behold,

I am against you, O Gog, prince of Rosh, Meshech and Tubal. I will turn you about and put hooks into your jaws, and I will bring you out, and all your army, horses and horsemen, all of them splendidly attired, a great company with buckler and shield, all of them wielding swords; Persia, Ethiopia and Put with them, all of them with shield and helmet; Gomer with all its troops; Beth-togarmah from the remote parts of the north with all its troops—many peoples with you'" (Ezekiel 38:1-6).

Of course, none of the place names in Ezekiel 38:1-6 exist on any modern map. Ezekiel used ancient place names that were familiar to the people of his day. While the names of these geographical locations have changed many times throughout history and may change again, the geographical territory remains the same. Regardless of what names they may carry at the time of this future invasion, it is these specific geographical areas that will be involved. The nations represented by these names today are Russia, Iran, the nations of central Asia, Turkey, Sudan, and Libya.

According to Ezekiel's astonishing prophecy, at the time of the invasion Israel will be at rest and living securely under its treaty with the Group of Ten. For this reason, Israel will let its guard down for the first time in its modern history.

After many days you will be summoned; in the latter years you will come into the land that is restored from the sword, whose inhabitants have been gathered from many nations to the mountains of Israel which had been a continual waste; but its people were brought out from the nations, and they are living securely, all of them...you will say, "I will go up against the land of unwalled villages. I will go against those who are at rest, that live securely, all of them living without walls and having no bars or gates…Therefore prophesy, son of man, and say to Gog, 'Thus says the Lord GOD, "On that day when My people Israel are living securely, will you not know it?"'" (Ezekiel 38:8,11,14).

According to the Bible, there are only two times in Israel's future that the nation will be at peace and rest. One of those times is during the millennial reign of Christ on the earth when the nations of the world will bask in the blessings of the Prince of Peace. But the invasion described by Ezekiel can't occur during that time because there will be no war in the millennium. The only other time Israel will be at peace is during the first three-and-a-half years of its treaty with the Antichrist. I believe that's when the events depicted in Ezekiel 38–39 will be fulfilled.

In one of the great surprise attacks of all time, a Russian leader will gather a group of what today are Islamic nations to attack Israel to wipe it off the face of the earth and steal its riches. This arrogant army will be supernaturally decimated by God in a dramatic display of divine judgment (Ezekiel 38:18–39:24). With the destruction of the Russian-Islamic power bloc, a huge power vacuum will be created, and the balance of power will swing decisively to the world's new strongman. As Satan's man of the hour, he will then attempt to destroy Israel, now disarmed and at peace (Daniel 7:25; 11:41).

8. The World Dictator Fills the Vacuum

The world leader, who heads the G-10, will break his covenant with Israel after three-and-a-half years (Daniel 9:27). He will declare himself world dictator, and in the fashion of the Babylonian and Roman emperors, he will deify himself, command the worship of the world, and set up an image of himself in a rebuilt temple in Jerusalem (2 Thessalonians 2:4). The Bible calls him the Antichrist (1 John 2:18) and the beast (Revelation 13:1-10). Unrivaled political, economic, and religious power will be centralized in one man. He will establish his "mark" as the requirement for people to engage in any form of commerce. He will exercise absolute control over global supply and demand. His world commerce secretary, known in the Bible as the false prophet or beast from the earth (Revelation 13:11-18), will lead the world in the worship of the world leader and implement the infamous mark of the beast (666). These earthshaking events will usher in the time that Jesus called the Great Tribulation—the final three-and-a-half years of this age (Matthew 24:21).

9. The March to Armageddon

Topping all the other disasters of the end times, a world war of unprecedented proportions will come. Armies from all over the earth will gather for a gigantic world power struggle centered at a place called Armageddon, or Mount Megiddo, which overlooks an expansive valley in northern Israel (Revelation 16:13-16). The area will become the scene of the conflict of the ages. Millions will perish in this greatest war of all history.

10. The Glorious Appearing

Before the war is resolved and the victor determined, Jesus Christ will come back in power and glory from heaven along with millions of angels and raptured Christians. His coming is described in graphic terms in Revelation 19. Coming as the King of kings and judge of the world, He will destroy the contending armies and bring in His own kingdom of peace and righteousness on earth.

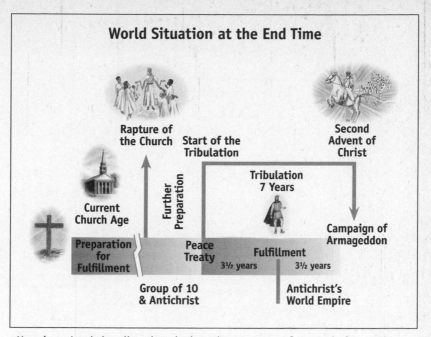

Here is a visual time line that depicts the sequence of events before and during the Tribulation.

Adapted and used with permission of Tim LaHaye and Thomas Ice, *Charting the End Times* (Eugene, OR: Harvest House, 2001). The chart above is based on charts that appear in LaHaye and Ice's book, with one adaptation: the placement of the Group of 10 and Antichrist before the signing of the peace treaty rather than after.

After reading this brief overview of the end times, doesn't it look like the pieces are coming together for the final act? Key players are taking their predicted places. Ancient prophecies will be fulfilled. And among other things, the nations will rush toward a one-world cashless economic system.

3

YOUR FUTURE IS IN THE CARDS

From Paper to Plastic

> *"It's one of those vast social upheavals that everyone understands but that hardly anyone notices, because it seems too ordinary: the long-predicted 'cashless society' has quietly arrived, or nearly so; currency, coins and checks are receding as ways of doing everyday business; we've become Plastic Nation. In the tangled history of American money—from tobacco receipts to gold and silver coins to paper money and checks— this is a seismic shift. Time to pay attention."*
>
> ROBERT SAMUELSON

You've probably seen the Visa commercials that have been nationally broadcast that hail the use of plastic and mock the use of cash. I've seen three versions of the ad. One commercial has a rollicking version of Louis Armstrong singing "When the Saints Go Marching In" while a bunch of New Orleans Saints football fans get ready for game day by buying lots of stuff at a sports store. One by one they lay down their Visa cards to purchase their paraphernalia. These are real men. Real sports fans. Real Americans. Then a guy wearing a pink shirt and a sweater tied around his neck— obviously an outdated preppy—steps up to buy some tennis balls. It's obvious that he's clueless. But his real crime? He pays with cash instead of plastic. The music stops as the vendor gives him a "What, are you kidding me?" look and begrudgingly hands the customer his change. Then the guy leaves, the music kicks back in, and the real football fans can get back to buying stuff with Visa. The ad ends with the now-familiar words, "Visa makes it easier for fans to get ready for game day. Life takes Visa."[1]

Another commercial titled "Lunch," is set in a crowded food court at lunchtime with people busily obtaining their food and drinks with the timing and precision of a factory assembly line. The music is upbeat and fast-paced. One after another the customers receive their order, swipe their Visa card and move on—with no signature required. The engine of commerce hums flawlessly. That is, until a man dares to hand the checkout lady a few well-worn dollar bills for his food. Everything comes to a dead stop, including the music. Chaos ensues. Trays of food fall to the floor, drinks spill, and the line comes to a screeching halt. There's dead silence. The other customers glare at him in disgust. His "foolish" decision to use cash has clogged the well-oiled gears of progress. He quickly moves on, the next man in line swipes his card, and the music revs back up. At the end of the commercial, a narrator states, "The Visa check card—because money shouldn't slow you down. Life takes faster money. Life takes Visa."

The third commercial features a bunch of hip young people dancing their way toward a checkout counter. Upbeat music is playing. The same basic scenario from the other two commercials is played out. But this time the narrator says, "Life takes beat, life takes rhythm, life takes Visa."

These commercials are a window into the current climate of how people transact business. More and more, cash is giving way to cashless means of payment. My wife was out shopping not long ago and went to a popular store in our city late in the afternoon. She told me that the checkout clerk who helped her commented that she was the first person all day who had used cash. The age of cashless transactions is here.

Show Me the Money

According to *Marketing Daily,* "Cash accounts for 20 percent of all consumer spending, credit cards for 25 percent, and debit cards for 12 percent, according to David Robertson, publisher of *The Nilson Report.* (The remaining 43 percent is paid for by other means, including checks, money orders, food stamps, cashier's checks, traveler's checks, official checks, remote electronic payments, and preauthorized electronic payments).[2] Robert Samuelson notes the quantum increase in using plastic over paper.

> You can use a card almost anywhere. From 1999 to 2005, the number of card-swiping terminals nearly tripled to 6.8 million, says the consulting firm Frost & Sullivan. Habits and mind-sets change. In 1990, most Americans regarded paying for groceries by credit card as unnatural. Now cards cover about 65 percent of food sales, says the Food Marketing Institute. There's electronic banking (83 percent of Social Security beneficiaries receive their monthly payments by automatic deposit), Internet buying, prepaid cards and automatic identity tags for toll booths.[3]

The total amount of U.S. currency in circulation (dollar bills of all amounts) is consistently dropping. In 1970, the economy's relative need for cash was almost twice as high as it was in 2006. The obvious reason for this drop is that more and more people are going cashless. Debit card use has soared in the United States over the last few years. As recently as 1996, cash and checks accounted for about 80 percent of consumer payments. It's now less than half that, and electronic payments are expected to exceed 70 percent of consumer payments by 2010. According to the Federal Reserve, from a peak of almost 50 billion in 1995, the number of checks written in the United States fell to 36.6 billion in 2003, while the number of electronic payments rose from 15 billion to 44 billion and continues to rise dramatically.[4] The Internet contains thousands of Web sites and articles announcing the trend from cash to cards.[5]

- "Visa Study: Majority of Baby Boomers and Echo Boomers See a Cashless Society"

- "AT&T Smart Cards May Become World Standard for Cashless Wallets, Electronic Commerce"

- "MasterCard, Cadbury-Schweppes to offer cashless vending machines"

- "CBS Television Features USA Technologies in Special Report on Cashless Vending; Philadelphia Nation's First City Targeted to Offer Credit/Debit Card Vending"

- "Federal Reserve Decision Expected to Accelerate Adoption of Cashless Technology in Vending and Other Small Ticket Cashless POS Markets"

There are more than 2 billion—yes that's billion with a *b*—credit and debit cards in the United States alone. Experts say there are about seven credit cards for every person over the age of 15.[6] The nature of how we pay for things is already changing drastically, but this is just a fraction of what's to come. It is estimated that by 2020, only 10 percent of financial transactions will be in cash. "We can safely predict that the idea of money as a physical object might well become extinct not long after, especially if a global pandemic starts us thinking about all the germs on those grubby notes. Instead, digital transactions will be made through computers, or cell phones, or even chips inserted into our forearms."[7] According to *Forbes,*

> Money is becoming much more of a concept than a physical entity, and most ordinary mortals haven't really noticed the switch. People are using credit and debit cards in more and more everyday situations, from meals purchased at fast-food restaurants and fuel purchased at gas stations to movies, groceries, sundries, highway tolls and clothing. Even New York City taxicabs are rigged with electronic card readers.
>
> Increasingly, paychecks are electronically deposited, and the money for the bills they pay—mortgages, utilities, cable and phone—are paid electronically as well. Banks offer incentives to consumers for using these direct-pay options, which allow them to keep better tabs on their customers and their money. Welfare and food stamps are issued on cards, which can be downloaded at the register or through an automatic teller machine.[8]

In 2007, Wal-Mart launched its store-branded reloadable money cards. The prepaid Visa debit cards have experienced increasing demand. By the summer of 2008, Wal-Mart had issued one million cards with a total of $1 billion loaded on them. The goal is to double that amount by the summer of 2009. Customers can reload their cards with a direct deposit and can also use the card to pay bills and shop anywhere that Visa debit cards are accepted.[9]

All of this is transforming our lives and society, but it is also paving the way for the cashless system of the final world ruler, the Antichrist, and his one-world financial system. Years ago, one of the best-known credit cards had a popular slogan: "Membership has its privileges." The end-time cashless system will also have its privileges. The mark of the beast will guarantee privileges to those who take its membership in the global society of the end times—primarily the ability to engage in commerce.

"Unshopping"

To give you a small glimpse of the kind of technology that exists, here are some new inventions that are already available that make many aspects of shopping and using cash obsolete or at least unnecessary. It's a line of innovations that boggle the mind. And this is just the beginning of what will develop in the next decade.[10]

Veggie Tales

Here's an item for all those who hate those slow checkout lines at the market: "For shoppers still trekking to the grocery store, IBM's Veggie Vision software can identify their produce by sight at the checkout, even through a plastic bag. No more fumbling to enter a label code or waiting for the cashier. Soon you might be able to skip checkout altogether."[11]

McCashless

This is already being tested at one McDonald's in South Korea: Customers with special software on their cell phones can receive the restaurant's updated menu as they walk through the door. While in line or even while seated, customers can point their phones at a menu and transmit their order to the counter. They then receive a text message when their order is ready, grab the food, and take a seat. And get this: McDonald's simply adds the cost of the food to the customer's cell phone bill.[12]

Intellifit

In the future, body-scanning software will allow you to create a virtual image of yourself to help with online clothes shopping. With this software, you can create your virtual counterpart, which will share the same physical dimensions as your real-world self. You can then use this virtual counterpart to "try on" the clothes you see in an online catalog. That way, you'll have a better idea of how clothes will actually fit you, as opposed to some model in a catalog. A company called Intellifit has "a booth that performs a 360-degree holographic scan of your fully clothed body."[13] The scan produces a detailed printout of the results, which you can then use to try on clothes from catalogs to see what they will look like on you.

Not Your Father's Ice Box

Even refrigerators are now available with a touch screen that allows you to watch television, play a DVD, display recipes, and even get the weather forecast. But that's nothing compared to the model Samsung plans to roll out soon. It uses "radio technology to inventory the contents of your fridge, alert you when expiration dates draw near, send shopping lists to your mobile phone, and possibly even place orders at your local market."[14] It will allow you to buy without ever shopping.

Everyone's Doing It

Between such inventions and the trend away from cash, the implementation of a cashless system would be fairly simple. Some kind of one-world currency could be required, but I don't believe that would be necessary. All we need is for everyone to agree (or be forced) to have their paycheck direct-deposited. This is no big deal. As of 2007, over 80 percent of all Social Security and SSI beneficiaries received their checks by direct deposit.[15] And according to a recent survey, over half (57 percent) of all Americans say that direct deposit is very important to managing their finances on a daily basis.[16]

Think about your own financial transactions:

- Do you use direct deposit for your paychecks?
- Do you use automatic, electronic withdrawal to pay your bills?
- How many credit cards do you have?
- Do you use a debit card instead of cash?
- Have you used a credit card for groceries?
- Do you swipe a card at the gas pump to save time?
- Have you used a credit card even for purchases of less than five dollars?
- How often do you give out your credit card number for Internet purchases?

Most of us are regularly engaged in many, if not all, of the kinds of transactions listed above on a regular basis. Of course, there is nothing inherently wrong with any these activities. In fact, they are often helpful time-savers. However, it's easy to see how all of them can move us ever closer to a cashless society.

Get Smart

The easy and natural next step would be to issue some kind of "smart card" that everyone can use to make all their purchases. Again, this is no stretch. People are already accustomed to using cards to buy everything from gas to bread. The smart card would be individualized and initialized to prevent unauthorized use. There are all kinds of methods already available for doing this, such as fingerprints, eye scan, a microchip or some other means of biometric scan, or a secret number. And with all the advanced technology available today, imagine what kinds of further mind-blowing ideas await us on the horizon!

A smart card looks like a credit card, only it's a little thicker. It's called *smart* because it is basically a computer disk that stores information about you.

> A smart card is a device that includes an embedded integrated circuit chip (ICC) that can be either a secure microcontroller or equivalent intelligence with internal memory or a memory chip alone. The card connects to a reader with direct physical contact or with a remote contactless radio frequency interface. With an embedded microcontroller, smart cards have the unique ability to store large amounts of data, carry out their own on-card functions (e.g., encryption and mutual authentication) and interact intelligently with a smart card reader. Smart card technology…is available in a variety of form factors,

including plastic cards, fobs, subscriber identification modules (SIMs) used in GSM mobile phones, and USB-based tokens.[17]

There are two basic kinds of smart cards: contact and contactless. The main difference, as you can see by the names, is that one requires insertion into a smart card reader, while the other requires only close proximity to a reader. With the proximity cards, all you have to do is wave the card in front of a reader and goods are paid for instantly—no signatures, no hassles. Several large companies have already jumped on the bandwagon and launched programs to gauge the effectiveness of the contactless technology.[18]

Smart cards have many applications worldwide, including:

- Secure identity applications—employee ID badges, citizen ID documents, electronic passports, driver's licenses, online authentication devices

- Healthcare applications—citizen health ID cards, physician ID cards, portable medical records cards

- Payment applications—contact and contactless credit/debit cards, transit payment cards

- Telecommunications applications—GSM Subscriber Identity Modules, pay telephone payment cards[19]

Joseph Schuler, a Maryland consultant, said this in *The Wall Street Journal:*

Smart cards' time has finally come. In the U.S., we're finally beginning to see some of the applications we thought we'd see three or four years ago. Millions of us already use these smart cards. For example, many college students purchase cards that operate soda, photocopy, or laundry machines. In Europe, many phone booths require smart cards. The idea behind these cards is simple. We buy, say, $10 worth of electronic money from a machine or a sales clerk. This $10 is stored on a plastic card and is electronically diminished every time we purchase something. In other words, the card has a memory.[20]

The move away from cash is nothing new or unexpected. Over a decade ago the cashless society was already moving quickly forward. "Our society is clearly moving towards an era when cash is no longer the most common form of payment. Smart cards will be the standard currency of this cashless society. Just as credit cards have replaced cash for large-value transactions in many parts of the world over the last 30 years, smart cards are likely to replace cash for many smaller transactions."[21] Back in 1995, Microsoft owner Bill Gates already envisioned a time when a wallet-sized personal computer will replace your cash.[22] And he ought to know.

The Stage Is Set

We are all aware of the financial problems in our world, the dramatic shift toward more government control and globalism, and the simultaneous move toward a cashless system. But what does it mean? Terry Cook, an expert on modern technology, suggests the following:

> The New World Order economists are not ignorant of the importance of cash and its ability to inhibit their total control of the world. They are aware that in order to completely control, track, and monitor the global

population, they must first eliminate the use of cash. With cash, there is no way to know how people are using their finances, whether for or against the government and its agenda. Because control of one's finances in essence means control of one's entire life, advocates of world government have for decades been promoting a move toward cashless transactions via a myriad of banking plans, ATM machines, credit cards, point-of-sale machines, credit data—all funneled through massive computer systems. Eventually the goal is control of all these computers by the economic leaders of the New World Order.[23]

The late Reverend Jerry Falwell, in a televised sermon from Thomas Road Baptist Church on August 27, 2006, saw where it's all headed:

> I expect a global economy in the twenty-first century, which first will manifest itself as a cashless society. I believe that plastic will take the place of cash, and that while this will only be fulfilled during the Tribulation period at the rapture, I believe that God is setting the stage for, and laying the infrastructure for, a cashless society right now. Most people...pay their bills online already. And the day will come, I believe, when there will be no cash, and the only way you can get cash and trade and do business is to have the mark of the beast.

Cashless is the wave of the future. It's the wave of today. What we see today points toward the advent of the final world ruler and his global financial system.

4

THE COMING CASHLESS SOCIETY

The Buck Stops Here

"Cashless Society*: A society in which all bills and debits
are paid by electronic money media, for example, bank
and credit cards, direct debits, and online payments."*
BNET BUSINESS DICTIONARY

*"No one, least of all in the press—least of all in the business
press—has seen the beginnings of what may be the greatest
revolution in the history of commerce: the end of money."*
THOMAS PETZINGER, JR.

*"Paying for goods with notes and coins could be
consigned to history within five years."*
CHIEF EXECUTIVE OF VISA EUROPE (2007)

In 1887, Edward Bellamy, a lawyer from western Massachusetts,
wrote his classic Utopian novel *Looking Backward: From 2000*

to 1887. It was the most celebrated utopian novel of the nineteenth century and the third-highest bestseller of its day, trailing only *Uncle Tom's Cabin* and *Ben Hur.*

The book tells the story of Julian West, a young Bostonian who falls into a deep, hypnosis-induced sleep in 1887 and wakes up 113 years later in the year 2000 in the same place but in a radically changed world. While he was sleeping, the United States became a socialist utopia. Mr. West quickly finds a reliable guide named Dr. Leete, who shows him around Boston in the year 2000 and explains all the advances of this new age, including the elimination of greed, misery, and war. West also learns about drastically reduced working hours even for menial jobs and the nearly instantaneous delivery of products from stores to homes. In this new world, there is universal retirement at age 45 with full benefits.

While there are all kinds of interesting predictions from Bellamy about what would happen by the year 2000, the most interesting one to me is that he predicted a massive socialistic system in which the government controls everything, a cashless society, and the universal use of credit cards. Bellamy narrates the following statements by Dr. Leete and Julian West:

> "As to the bankers, having no money we have no use for those gentry."

> "Another item wherein we save is the disuse of money and the thousand occupations connected with financial operations of all sorts."

> "Money was unknown and without conceivable use."[1]

Bellamy then provides this incredibly futuristic dialogue between Dr. Leete and Julian West:

A system of direct distribution from the national store-houses took the place of trade, and for this money was unnecessary. "How is this distribution managed?" I asked. "On the simplest possible plan," replied Dr. Leete. "A credit corresponding to his share of the annual product of the nation is given to every citizen on the public books at the beginning of each year, and a credit card issued him with which he procures at the public store-houses, found in every community, whatever he desires whenever he desires it. This arrangement, you will see, totally obviates the necessity for business transactions of any sort between individuals and consumers. Perhaps you would like to see what our credit cards are like... this card is issued for a certain number of dollars. We have kept the old word, but not the substance. The term, as we use it, answers to no real thing, but merely serves as an algebraic symbol for comparing the values of products with one another. For this purpose they are all priced in dollars and cents, just as in your day. The value of what I procure on this card is checked off by the clerk, who pricks out of these tiers of squares the price of what I order.[2]

What Bellamy prognosticated about credit cards is already here. Could his prediction of a cashless society also be on the horizon? It looks that way. Times are changing more rapidly than ever before, and the concept of a cashless society has been seriously advocated in the United States for almost 40 years. It's becoming the tsunami wave of the future. Consider these headlines:

"The Cashless Society Has Arrived" (*Real Clear Politics,* June 20, 2007)

"Cashless Society by 2012, says VISA chief" (*The Independent*, March 11, 2007)

"The Cashless Society: Buddy Can You Spare Me a Card-Swipe" (*Pink Slip* [blog], March 7, 2007)

"Our Cashless Future" (*The Futurist*, May-June 2007)

"E-zer pass eyed for cashless tolls" (*New York Post*, January 24, 2009)

"Will Canada be the first cashless society?" (canada.com, June 23, 2006)

"The End of the Cash Era" (*The Economist*, February 17-23, 2007—The cover pictures a graphic of dinosaurs made out of coins and bills. In an editorial, the magazine acknowledges that the trend of electronic payments replacing cash transactions is unstoppable.)

"The Vanishing Greenback" (*Newsweek*, June 25, 2007)

"Toll Roads Take Cashless Route" (*USA Today*, July 28, 2008)

"Coke pushes to keep up with cashless society" (*ContactlessNews*, August 10, 2007)

In June 2007, *Newsweek* featured a story by Robert Samuelson about the end of cash. He said, "If you visit the U.S. Bureau of Engraving and Printing (one operation in Washington, the other in Ft. Worth, Texas), you can still see greenbacks being made. They come off the presses in sheets of 32. In fiscal 2007, the government will print about 9.1 billion individual bills. But 95 percent is to replace worn currency, not to expand the supply. The Buck Starts Here, say signs on some printing presses. In reality, today's buck usually begins (and ends) as a mere data entry." Start taking notice, and you will see these kinds of headlines and articles more and more as cashless transactions become more and more a global reality.

"We are now cashless."

Normally, like many people, I don't listen carefully to what flight attendants say as they robotically go through their preflight spiel. However, on September 25, 2008, on a Southwest Airlines flight from Oklahoma City to Dallas, my ears perked up as I heard the flight attendant announce, "We are now a cashless cabin." At first her statement didn't sink in, but then she went on to explain that the airline no longer accepts cash for beer, wine, or liquor. Wow! Southwest Airlines is now cashless. I went to the airline's Web site and found this announcement:

> If you've been on a Southwest flight, you've no doubt heard the Flight Attendant ask for change for a $20 bill. Well, those days are going the way of knee socks and penny loafers (did I just date myself?). Beginning September 9, Southwest will "flip the switch" and accept only credit and debit cards for beer, liquor, and energy drink purchases.

Since then I've noticed that each Southwest Airlines attendant carries a small electronic credit card scanner for processing drink orders. Other airlines have followed suit. According to *The New York Times,*

> American Airlines is joining the growing number of airlines with cashless cabins. Starting this summer,

American will begin accepting only credit and debit cards for items like headsets and alcoholic beverages purchased onboard domestic and Canada flights. Other airlines that have gone cashless include Southwest, Alaska Airlines, JetBlue, AirTran, Virgin America and Midwest Airlines. Cash-only holdouts include Northwest, Continental and United. Delta and US Airways accept both cards and cash. Both United and US Airways have recently tested credit-only options on domestic flights.[3]

United Airlines officially went cashless in March 2009.[4] But cashless is not just in the United States or on airplanes, it's debuting all over the world and in ways most people have never dreamed.

Monopoly Goes Cashless

Growing up, almost everyone has played a hard-nosed game of Monopoly, working feverishly to drive their family members and friends into bankruptcy. My two sons and my dad love to play the game. They've enjoyed many evenings of strenuous competition. Up to now, the first thing game participants had to do was distribute a certain amount of money to each player before the game started. Those colorful $500 and $100 bills always impressed me as a young boy and stirred up feelings of greed and competition. But that Monopoly money is quickly becoming a childhood memory. That's right—even beloved Monopoly, the popular American board game, is on the cashless bandwagon. Monopoly is introducing a new version that ditches cash:

> Remember playing Monopoly as a kid? Getting scammed on a lousy deal by your weasely dad is a rite of passage,

as is having to hand over stacks of precious orange $100 bills after falling victim to his cruel hotel empire. Well, apparently your memories are outdated. This is the 21st century! No one uses cash anymore, it isn't extreme or flashy enough. At least that's what Parker Brothers says, as it's phasing out cash from its Monopoly sets, replacing it with an electronic debit card system.[5]

Monopoly is changing with the times.

While Monopoly is the paragon of good 'ole fashioned board game fun, the "old fashioned" part had to go. Parker Brothers is phasing out the cash-based version's fun money and replacing it with an "Electronic Banking" flavor that could leave Mr. Moneybags turning his pockets inside out as his stash is replaced by a magnetic strip. New kits are completely devoid of the famous multi-colored bills; instead, you'll find phony Visa debit cards and a calculator/reader which keeps a running tabulation of your riches—or lack thereof. A deal was struck with Visa to design the mock cards and readers, presumably after surveys showed that 70% of adults used cash less often now than they did a decade ago (no surprise there). When asked about the dramatic change, Parker said replacing cash with plastic "showed the game was moving with the times."[6]

Monopoly is now equipped with a scanner that players swipe their cards through to debit or credit money. Who would have ever believed this would happen? The British version of the game, Monopoly Here & Now Electronic Banking, went on sale in 2006. When Monopoly goes cashless, you know that the rest of society can't be far behind.

RFID

It looks like the beloved greenback is going the way of eight-track tapes, cassette tapes, and VHS tapes. Already, unimaginable technology is being tested and implemented that will change forever the way we pay for services or goods. One of these applications is RFID (Radio Frequency Identification) technology. RFID is already in use all around us. If you have ever used EZPass through a toll booth, or paid for gas using SpeedPass, you've used RFID. It's increasingly used with biometric technologies for security purposes. In the near future you could go shopping at The Gap and purchase a pair of jeans, and then the next time you enter the store you would be immediately identified by RFID technology. Pretty cool or pretty spooky, depending on your perspective.

RFID technology is being proposed for businesses to help monitor productivity and activity by workers. A simple RFID-enabled system can track how long certain jobs take as well as trail where employees go and how long they are there. It can also help retailers track shipping, delivery, and inventory.

RFID can be placed in smart cards or even in cell phones. RFID is similar to bar codes that now appear on products everywhere. However, one of the key differences between RFID and bar code technology is "RFID eliminates the need for line-of-sight reading that bar coding depends on. Also, RFID scanning can be done at greater distances than bar code scanning."[7] High-frequency RFID systems can function at distances up to 90 feet away and can be read through the human body or clothing.

A basic RFID system consists of three components:

- An antenna or coil

- A transceiver (with decoder)
- A transponder (RF tag) electronically programmed with unique information

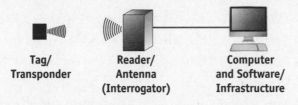

Tag/	Reader/	Computer
Transponder	Antenna	and Software/
	(Interrogator)	Infrastructure

And here is how it works:

- The antenna emits radio signals to activate the tag and to read and write data to it.
- The reader emits radio waves in ranges of anywhere from one inch to 100 feet or more, depending upon its power output and the radio frequency used. When an RFID tag passes through the electromagnetic zone, it detects the reader's activation signal.
- The reader decodes the data encoded in the tag's integrated circuit (silicon chip) and the data is passed to the host computer for processing.[8]

Eventually, anything you buy that's more expensive than a pack of gum will carry an RFID tag instead of a bar code. And if you have a plastic card or cell phone fitted with RFID, you will never even have to take it out of your pocket to pay for the item. Every product you purchase at the store would be automatically registered to your account via computer processing.

Rise of the Machines

The move toward a cashless society has even arrived at the most basic American icon—the vending machine. In many places vending machines are going cashless. The new machines are called Intelligent Vending Machines (IVM). SkyeTek, Inc., the leading provider of embedded RFID reader technology, has developed the first consumer application for RFID. In partnership with Isochron, Inc., SkyeTek has enabled cashless payment at vending machines located throughout the Hartsfield-Jackson Atlanta International Airport. Consumers equipped with RFID-enabled credit cards can now make a purchase by just waving a card within a few feet of the new vending machines.[9] Coca-Cola bottlers are using IVMs around the world. This same wireless technology is being applied to everything—ticket sales, laundromats, public phones, vending machines, and automated kiosks. With the click of a bluetooth-enabled mobile phone, consumers can now shop without physical cash. You can leave your wallet at home.[10]

Cashless Makes Cents

Major changes in the way we do things usually don't happen until there's a perceived need or a crisis that demands action. Change is usually slow to come unless that change creates a distinct advantage over the status quo. Of course, this raises the question: Why would the economies of the world go cashless? What are the justifications and advantages of adopting a cashless system? Is it a time saver or a trap? A help or hindrance? Is the versatility, security, and convenience worth the price people would pay in loss of privacy? A growing number of people say yes. Consider these six key advantages to a cashless society.

Greater Security

According to *USA Today,* there's been an alarming spike in identify theft in the wake of the global financial crisis. Identity theft is definitely a major inconvenience and headache for the victims because it can take years to straighten out the mess with uncooperative credit companies, banks, and even legal authorities. As Robert Samuelson notes, "We have crossed a cultural as well as an economic threshold when plastic and money are synonyms and the crime of choice is identity theft, not bank robbery."[11] A method that develops a foolproof global identity system would be invaluable, saving thousands of man-hours and millions or even billions of dollars. The development and implementation of a cashless system based on some kind of biometric means of verification would make the current flood of identity theft a historical footnote.

Another compelling argument for pursuing a worldwide digital monetary system is the fight against international crime, especially terrorism. Digital money, unlike cash, is traceable. This would help cut off the financial lifeline for terror cells all over the globe.

Welcomed Convenience

In a cashless society, retailers wouldn't have to worry about bounced checks, credit checks, looking at IDs, or even checking customers out at a cash register. A shopper could gather the items she wants and simply walk out the door with the purchases automatically debited from her RFID credit card or cell phone.

Decrease in Crime

Going cashless would eliminate muggings, convenience- and liquor-store robberies, and bank heists. No one can steal cash from an Intelligent Vending Machine. It wouldn't even make sense for a crook to force you to transfer money to his card because the trans-action would be electronically recorded and easily traceable back to the perpetrator. A cash-free society would also drive a stake in the heart of illegal drug trade. Drug traffickers and users could no longer slither under the radar of law enforcement authorities. The cash-dependent drug trade would dry up.

Less Expensive

Another benefit of a cashless society is that it's less expensive. Printing, handling, storing, and securing all those greenbacks isn't cheap.

Cash is expensive. Huh? That's right:

> We've got an economy out there that is melting before our eyes and yet we insist on traveling to the bank once a week, and buying things with cash money. In fairness, though, we have made progress. We are not visiting the bank quite as much, which reduces their costs which in turn is good for us customers. But, instead we are vis-iting ATM machines where we are getting—CASH!!! What's the alternative? Technology! Technology in the form of electronic payment devices—cash cards, debit cards, antenna'd devices, or even cell phones! The cost of using technology for financial transactions is far less than the cost of dealing with money—money costs money to make, store, distribute, and bank. Technol-ogy costs virtually nothing other than the price of the gadgets involved.[12]

Going cashless would also allow banks and retailers to reduce their workforce by laying off bank tellers, retail clerks, and book-keepers, and they could then pass on the savings to customers.

Eliminating Counterfeiting

The Secret Service was created in 1865 by Abraham Lincoln to deal with a national crisis: one-third of the nation's money at the time was counterfeit. That's correct—33 percent. Today it's a far cry from that, standing at .02 percent. However, that's still a sizable amount. According to the Secret Service, $103 million of fake money was removed from circulation from October 2007 to August 2008. And there are fears the situation could easily get much worse as sophisticated new optical scanning technologies become available.

Every year since 1985, the editors of *The Futurist* have selected the key forecasts for the future and put them in an annual Outlook Report. The number four forecast in Outlook 2008 is "Counterfeiting of currency will proliferate, driving the move toward a cashless society."

Disease-Free

For society to go cashless would reap substantial medical benefits. Let's face it: Paper money is dirty. It's a magnet for bacteria and viruses. In a world more and more concerned about the outbreak of deadly plagues and pandemics, eliminating the endless handling and exchange of cash could help short-circuit the spread of deadly diseases.

Easy to Replace

Think of all the people every day who lose their wallets or cash due to carelessness, forgetfulness, home fires, or theft. A lost or melted cash card or cell phone can be quickly and easily replaced. That is not true about cash.

Stimulus Package

The U.S. government knows that millions of Americans operate outside the recognized economy. Many run family businesses or accept cash payments only, and do not report their earnings to the IRS. Total reliance upon a money card or cashless system would allow the IRS to tax this underground economy, adding billions of dollars into the tax coffers. A cash-free market could rescue our nation economically. In their bestselling book *Are We Living in the End Times?* Tim LaHaye and Jerry Jenkins note:

> Do governments want this technology to be compulsory? Absolutely! In America alone, millions of people are doing business under the table on a cash-only basis in order to bypass the enormous tax rate. Eliminating this possibility could net the United States treasury an estimated 200 billion to a trillion additional dollars a year. Just think how fast the national debt could be paid with an increase of close to a trillion a year in currently unpaid taxes…Look soon for the government to begin calling for legislation to do away with cash.[13]

With the U.S. Treasury $11 trillion in debt and bailouts galore, this new source of cash could certainly look like an attractive option to the U.S. government. Of course, the government will fail to mention the drawbacks of this system, such as restrictions on freedom and privacy. The cashless system will mark the official death of freedom because, when you stop and think about it, financial control equals total control. When the cashless society becomes reality, "Big Brother" won't be far behind. He will know everything about you! As LaHaye and Jenkins powerfully point out: "And national 'Big Brother' is just one step away from 'International Big Brother'—the number of his name is 666!"[14]

Your Cellphone—Don't Leave Home Without It

The four main tools of the coming cashless society are credit cards, debit cards, smart cards, and cell phones. We are all familiar with credit and debit cards, and we discussed smart cards briefly in the last chapter. But the *real* future of the coming cashless society is right in your hand or pocket. It's now widely believed that the cell phone you carry with you everywhere will ultimately replace even your credit cards. It will be the digital wallet of the future.

Many people today have their cell phone with them 24/7. They carry it with them even as they are horseback riding, roller skating, sitting in church, or doing just about any other activity you can think of. The cell phone has become ubiquitous. Its availability transcends economic boundaries, and it has become the beacon of modern-day society.

Not long ago I was watching a program on television that featured a segment that had something to do with Africa. As I casually looked on, I suddenly noticed something that I've never forgotten. Out in the middle of nowhere, surrounded by parched, cracked earth and a few emaciated cattle, stood a half-naked tribesman talking on a cell phone. Something about that picture just wasn't right. How did he get a cell phone? Who he was talking to? Where is his monthly bill sent? Then it struck me: Anyone, anywhere can now talk to anyone else anytime. Globalism, fueled by incredible technology, is here.

According to experts, cell phones are going to replace credit cards. They will also replace PCs as the primary gateway to the Internet. It's estimated that there are now about 2.6 billion cell phones in the world, and the number continues to skyrocket. Visa is actively exploring the use of cell phones or mobile payments.

BBC News carried an article in February 2009 titled "Challenges to a Cashless World," which reported that mobile phones will become the integral link to the coming cashless society. They believe this will become reality sometime in the next three to five years.

> Once you wouldn't leave home without it. But the credit card could soon be cashing in its chips. Experts predict that paying by plastic will make way for payments by mobile phone, key fob or even fingerprint. Like the cheque book, video cassette and CD before it, the plastic credit card could be on the way out within five years, according to leading financiers. Yesterday Barclaycard, which introduced the UK's first credit card in 1966, announced it was pouring millions into developing "contactless payment technology." The group has already developed a credit card that can be read without having to be taken out of a wallet. It hopes to take contactless payments a step further with chips that can be inserted into mobile phones, enabling shoppers to buy items by simply holding their handsets over them. The purchase would be confirmed by tapping a PIN into the phone, with no need to go to the checkout. There is even talk of customers paying by fingerprint or eye recognition in the future...The credit card company envisages customers being alerted to special offers in nearby shops through their mobiles, which they can then use to pay. The idea is that a customer could hold his handset over an item, such as a sandwich, to get the price and the number of calories displayed on the screen before deciding whether to buy.[15]

The Economist points to mobile phones as the ticket to the future of commerce.

Some of the hottest nightclubs have a new trick for checking the identity of their VIP guests: they send an entry pass in the form of a super barcode to their mobile phones. This is scanned by the large gentleman who lifts the velvet rope. Even those who must pay to get in may need their handsets: at a recent clubbers' night at London's Ministry of Sound, students were offered discounts if they used their mobile phones to buy electronic tickets. Mobile phones are becoming an increasingly popular way to make all sorts of payments. In America fans of the Atlanta Hawks have been testing specially adapted Nokia handsets linked to their Visa cards to enter their local stadium and to buy refreshments. Elsewhere schemes are more advanced. You can already pass the day in Austria without carrying cash, credit or debit cards by paying for everything, including consumer goods, with a mobile phone.[16]

It requires no sci-fi imagination or leap of faith to see where all of this is headed. As more advanced technology comes online, it in turn spawns more complex technology, and on and on. There are probably very few people today who have to be convinced that we're on the fast track to the technology of tomorrow. Cashless is coming. The issue is no longer *if* it's coming, but rather *when* it will come, and what kinds of technology will be used to implement it.

Cashless—the Heart of the Antichrist's System

Now, the Bible never explicitly says the coming one-world economic system will be a cashless system. It only says that people will have to need the beast's mark in order to transact business.

However, if cash is still king during the reign of Antichrist, it would be very difficult for him to control world commerce. Think about it: If people are still able to use cash, those who are without the mark could develop an extensive black market system that would allow them to secure goods and services. But if there is no cash available, people will have to use the mark to make payments. The absence of cash, and the adoption of some kind of electronic transaction system, would give the Antichrist the means to enforce his complete stranglehold on world commerce. The only option left to people outside his economic system would be bartering, and this would last only as long as people have things of value to trade. Make no mistake—if the Antichrist is to gain control over every sale or purchase, it appears cash must be eliminated so that there is a record of every transaction that takes place.

Does this mean we should resist the cashless trend and avoid using services such as direct deposit, electronic turnpike passes, or smart cards? Not necessarily. None of these uses are inherently evil in and of themselves. These new technologies are very convenient and make sense. But we do need to be aware of what is happening and how these changes may be setting the stage for what's to come. The bottom line is this: The coming cashless society is not immoral or evil, but it does serve as a sign that we're drawing closer to the end times.

Forty years ago, in 1970, the blockbuster best-seller *The Late Great Planet Earth* saw what was coming by looking through the lens of Bible prophecy:

> Do you believe it will be possible for people to be controlled electronically? In our computerized society, where we are all "numbered" from birth to death, it seems completely plausible that someday in the near future

the numbers racket will consolidate and we will have just one number for all our business, money, and credit transactions. Leading members of the business community are now planning that all money matters will be handled electronically.[17]

We see this coming true today right before our eyes.

One of the key challenges of going to a cashless system is making sure the person who is using the smart card or cell phone to make a transaction is the real owner. But ownership could be easily verified by the use of some kind of biometrics along with global positioning technology.

In fact, the biometrics that the beast could employ are quickly moving into place.

BIOMETRICS AND THE BEAST

Don't Let It Get Under Your Skin

*"Biometrics is the science and technology
of measuring and analyzing biological data.
In information technology, biometrics refers
to technologies that measure and analyze human
body characteristics, such as fingerprints, eye
retinas and irises, voice patterns, facial patterns and
hand measurements, for authentication purposes."*
INFORMATION SECURITY MAGAZINE

I was born in 1959. So, like many of you, I remember rotary-dial phones, cars without air conditioning, black-and-white television sets with rabbit-ear antennae and three channels, clotheslines, typewriters, eight-track stereos, cassette tapes, clunky mobile phones, and beta max. Who would have thought 30 years ago that a state-of-the-art electric typewriter would be a dust-collecting museum piece in a mere decade? Is it possible that in the near future, that prized "Benjamin" in your wallet will become a relic? That you will no longer hear the sound of change jingling in your pocket? That your children or grandchildren will grow up never knowing what money even looks or feels like? This may seem far-fetched, but it's not. Interest in the cashless society is growing by the day. Major plans are under way to make it a reality. When it comes, here are some expressions that will fall by the wayside:

- Spare change?
- Keep the change.
- Do you have change for a hundred?
- In for a dime, in for a dollar.
- Penny wise, pound foolish.
- There's not a dime's worth of a difference between x and y.
- A penny saved is a penny earned.
- That and a quarter will buy you—well, I guess this one's already fallen by the wayside, since a quarter won't buy you anything.
- All she sees are dollar signs.[1]

If experts are to be believed, cashless is just around the corner. But for it to really take off will require some sophisticated technology. Enter the world of biometrics—the science of identifying people based on unique physical characteristics. Cashless must be linked to some kind of biometrics. Biometric technology interfaces perfectly with a cashless society. After all, one of the key security issues of a cashless society and the use of some kind of smart card or your cell phone is ensuring that the person using the card or cell phone is the correct owner. The bottom-line issue in biometrics is, "Am I who I say I am?" Already, most laptops or PCs have some kind of fingerprint scanner to prevent unauthorized use. This same technology is being expanded for other uses.

The "Eyes" Have It

On May 14, 2007, MSNBC ran a story titled "The Future of Biometrics." It examined what life may look like in 2017. The story investigated new technology related to eye scans and reading faces, and reported that in Jewel Osco stores in Chicago, people are able to pay for their purchases using nothing more than their fingerprints. This technology is being tested all over the world, and because the potential applications are many, there's exponential growth in the imaging market. Besides fingerprints, other physiological biometrics are being considered, including face recognition, iris or retina scan, hand geometry, body odor, hand or finger veins, footprints, palm prints, and even tongue scanning. You may soon hear the words, "Open your mouth and say aah" at the checkout stand.

There are many common everyday uses in which biometrics could provide greater efficiency and enhance our lives, such as making it possible to unlock and start your car, to open the doors to your home and office, to access an account at a bank or ATM, turn on appliances or stereos, etc. You would not need access cards or keys—just your body as the means by which to gain access.

The Department of Motor Vehicles in California is trying to make biometrics a part of every person's driver's license. They want to implement thumbprint and facial-recognition technology for verifying the identity of applicants for new driver's licenses and state ID cards. It's hoped that this will help reduce the number of fraudulent driver's licenses used by people in the state. Several other states, including Texas, New Mexico, Oregon, and Georgia, have already implemented facial-recognition technology and are reporting success with it.[2] Once this type of data is stored, it could greatly enhance law enforcement efforts. It would allow law enforcement personnel to scan an entire crowd of people, check images against a database, and immediately have the names and addresses of the people in the crowd. Of course, this raises all kinds of Big Brother issues, but this technology could help get dangerous criminals off the streets.

In a world vulnerable to the threat of terrorism, biometrics may become a standard means of identification. Think how much safer and more convenient it would be to have digital scanning devices at airports. People who have preapproved clearance could be instantaneously identified by simply having them place their finger on a monitor or walk through a scanning device.

Getting Chippy

Another biometric application that would prevent fraud in the use of checks and credit cards is a syringe-injectable microchip implant.[3] For now, the chip implant, equipped with RFID technology, could be used to insure that whoever is writing a check or using a credit card is authorized to do so. Or it could be used to access important medical information. But in the future the implant could be upgraded to keep track of the transactions, movements, and location of every person.

Almost everyone today is familiar with the various kinds of chips that can be planted under the skin, often on the hand or the forearm. This technology is often viewed in connection with the mark of the beast in Revelation 13. Is it possible that some kind of implant will be the dreaded mark of the beast? We'll answer that question in chapter 11.

The Roadrunner

Given the number of people who live on earth—more than six billion—you may be asking, Is it really possible to store all of this biometric information in one place? Is such technology really viable on a global scale?

We now have superfast computers available that stagger the imagination. The world's fastest computer, nicknamed Road-runner, reached a monumental milestone recently. On May 26, 2008, at 3:30 a.m., the $133 million IBM supercomputer system at the Los Alamos National Laboratory broke the long-sought-after petaflop barrier. Like me, you're probably wondering what that means. The petaflop barrier is one quadrillion calculations per second. To put this in perspective, that's 150,000 calculations per second for every man, woman, and child on earth.

IBM has developed a new supercomputer called the Sequoia:

> With a speed of 20 petaflops—or 20,000 trillion calculations per second—Sequoia is expected to be the most powerful supercomputer in the world, IBM said, and will be approximately 10 times faster than today's most powerful system. To put this into perspective, if each of the 6.7 billion people on Earth had a hand calculator and worked together on a massive calculation for 24 hours per day, 365 days a year, it would take 320 years to do what Sequoia will do in one hour.[4]

Scientists are now shooting for the exaflop barrier. An exaflop is a million trillion calculations per second, or a quintillion. That's a thousand times faster than a petaflop. The prediction is that the exaflop barrier will be reached in 2019. There is no doubt that the technology is now available for us to store all the information that will be required for a one-world economic system as well as the biometric data to back it up.

Surveillance Society

Hollywood is fascinated with biometrics. From James Bond and *Charlie's Angels* to the team from *Mission Impossible,* there are many shows and movies that feature some kind of biometric technology. The hit movie *Minority Report,* starring Tom Cruise, came out in 2002. The movie was set in Washington, D.C. in the year 2054. *Minority Report* presents a society that seems, in many ways, a logical extension of our own. An online review of the movie says,

> The notion of privacy is a distant memory; our every movement can be tracked by retinal scanners, which are as ubiquitous as the holographic billboards that utilize them to personalize their advertising pitches. A Gap billboard, scanning a passing pedestrian, burbles "Greetings, Mr. Yakomoto! How are those tank tops working out for you?" Indeed, one of the most frightening things about this movie is the participation of real-life corporations like the Gap and Lexus, cheerfully lending their logos to these Orwellian ads and probably paying good money for the honor.[5]

In the movie, Tom Cruise even has his eyes surgically removed to evade detection via iris scans that are everywhere. But later he is able to re-enter his former workplace by holding his own extracted eyeballs against a scanner because the employer had forgotten to cancel his access rights! Biometrics may not be confined to the imagination of movie producers for long; they go hand in hand with a cashless society.

In their excellent book *Are We Living in the End Times?* Tim LaHaye and Jerry Jenkins note the significance of modern technology and the fulfillment of Revelation 13:

> Thinking people who read Revelation 13 have long wondered how the Antichrist could exercise such total control over billions of people. How could it be possible that they could not buy or sell without his mark? For the first time in two thousand years, it is now technologically possible to enforce such a system. Microchips have already been invented that can be placed in the fatty tissue behind the ear or in other places of the body to enable others to track that individual. (Such systems are already in place to track family pets.) We are all familiar with the scanner at the checkout counter of most stores. All it would take is a computer program that required the "666" number on people's accounts (or hands and foreheads) in order for them to "buy or sell." Mark-of-the-Beast technology is already here![6]

LaHaye and Jenkins conclude: "Still, technology by itself is nearly powerless. It will finally become prophetically potent in *the coming world-wide move to a cashless society*...The one-world planners are on a fast track toward a cashless society."[7]

Preview of Coming Attractions

The real bottom line on current technology, biometrics, and the current move toward a cashless society is not that any of it is inherently evil or sinful, but that these are signs of the times. When you go see a movie nowadays, the movie is preceded by a string of trailers or previews of upcoming films. The purpose of these teasers is to pique your interest in seeing those films when they're released. In much the same way, the technology around us provides a preview of life in the future. Yet sadly, the feature presentation will be far worse than any preview we can imagine today. After the rapture of true believers in Christ to heaven, the main show will unfold on earth as the seven-year Tribulation begins. The main actor in this drama will be the coming Antichrist, and the cashless society will be a key element of his plan for world dominion.

But before the Antichrist appears, the stage must be set. The rise of a group of ten leaders and an economic earthquake will pave the way for his entrance upon the world stage.

Rise of the G-10

The End-Time Economic System Begins

> "The new Europe is a more integrated place today
> than any time since the Roman Empire. The new
> United States of Europe…has more people, more
> wealth, and more trade than the United States."
>
> T.R. Reid
> Author, *The United States of Europe*

Everywhere one looks today, there's another group of nations being created to deal with the growing complexities and uncertainties of the world economy. There's the G-7, G-15, G-20, G-30, G-77, and a proposed G-33. Nations are forging necessary economic alliances to stay afloat and insure credit and available markets for their own benefit.

This development is compelling because, according to the Bible, the first key event after the rapture of true believers to heaven will be the formation of a reunited Roman Empire aligned under the rule of ten leaders, or what we might call the G-10. While the Bible never explains why these ten leaders come together, it's logical to conclude that they emerge to protect the political and economic interests of the West in the chaos that ensues after the rapture. They may well be the iron fist that stops the chaos after the rapture, insures the continued flow of oil, and stabilizes the world economy. Their emergence marks the first critical step on the road to the one-world economic system of the last days.

We're first introduced to the Bible's G-10 in the book of Daniel.

Ten Toes and Ten Horns

About 2500 years ago the Jewish prophet Daniel was given a panoramic revelation by God that revealed the sweep of world history from Daniel's day all the way up to the second coming of Jesus back to planet earth. Daniel wrote most of his great prophecy in the middle of the sixth century B.C., near the end of the 70-year Jewish exile in Babylon. During this time of discipline, God knew that His people would have all kinds of questions, such as, Is God finished with us? Will God be faithful to His covenant with Abraham to give us the land of Israel forever? Will the kingdom promised to David ever be realized? Will Messiah ever come to rule over the earth?

In Daniel 2 and 7, God encouraged His people and answered their questions by giving them an overview of the course of world history. God wanted them to know that His promises were sure and that He would keep His Word—and that the promised kingdom would eventually come to Israel. However, God also wanted them to know that the kingdom would not come immediately. Before the King and His kingdom would come, four great world empires would rule over Israel in succession. With the benefit of 20/20 hindsight, we now know that these four empires were Babylon, Medo-Persia, Greece, and Rome. In Daniel 2 these four empires are represented by four metals in a great statue that King Nebuchadnezzar saw in a dream.

The Statue in Daniel 2	
Head of gold	Babylon
Arms and chest of silver	Medo-Persia
Stomach and thighs of bronze	Greece
Legs of iron	Rome

Up to this point, almost everyone is in general agreement about the meaning of Nebuchadnezzar's dream in Daniel 2. But in Daniel 2:42-44, we read that the statue has feet and toes of iron and baked clay. This represents the final form of the Roman Empire, and the ten toes represent the ten kings who will rule simultaneously just before the return of Jesus back to earth to establish His kingdom.

In Daniel 7 these same world empires are pictured again, but this time as four wild beasts that Daniel saw rising up out of the Mediterranean Sea.

The Four Beasts in Daniel 7	
Winged lion	Babylon
Bloodthirsty bear	Medo-Persia
Leopard with four heads and two wings	Greece
Terrible beast	Rome

Just as in Daniel 2, the number ten appears in relation to the end of the final empire. In Daniel 2, we read about the ten toes of the image. In Daniel 7, we read about a terrible beast with ten horns (verse 7). The terrible beast corresponds to the legs of iron, and the ten horns correspond to the ten toes. So, the final phase of the Roman Empire is depicted by ten horns, which are identified as ten kings (Daniel 7:24). Many have interpreted these ten toes and ten horns as nations or regions into which the world will be divided in the end times. But Daniel 2:44 and 7:25 clearly identify them as kings or individuals who will form some kind of ruling committee. These ten leaders may represent various nations or groups of nations, but the Bible never says so specifically. What we are told is that they are ten leaders who will come together to form a reunited Roman Empire. These same ten end-time leaders are mentioned by the apostle John in Revelation 17:12-13, where again they are described as ten horns.

Interpreting the Future in Light of the Past

Some who read Daniel 2 and 7 believe that the ten toes and ten horns are already past—that they were part of the historical Roman Empire that was destroyed in A.D. 476. Yet we know from history that the Roman Empire never had a ten-king ruling body as required by both Daniel 2 and 7. Moreover, there is a complete, sudden destruction of the great image in Daniel 2 and the beast in Daniel 7. The image in Daniel 2 is suddenly smashed to pieces and the dust is blown away. But the Roman Empire gradually deteriorated and declined until the western part of the empire fell in A.D. 476 and the eastern leg was cut off in A.D. 1453. A more gradual process could hardly be imagined. With its slow decline the Roman Empire left unfulfilled the sudden destruction of the great statue and the terrible beast.

The principal reason for believing in the revival of the ancient Roman Empire is the simple fact that prophecy requires it. Prophecies dealing with the final phase of this empire have not been literally fulfilled in the same way as the prophecies about the first three world empires. To those who believe the Bible, the prophecies of the future are just as authentic as the prophecies already fulfilled in the past. One must conclude that a revival of the ancient Roman Empire—as described in the unfulfilled prophecies of Daniel—has not yet appeared on the stage of world history.

The future form of the Roman Empire, according to Daniel, will emerge prior to the coming of Christ to rule over the earth. This future manifestation will take the form of a coalition or confederation of ten world leaders (symbolized by the ten toes in Daniel 2 and the ten horns in Daniel 7) who have power over the same basic geographical territory as the original or historical Roman Empire. When Daniel presents these two forms of the Roman Empire, he skips over many centuries from historical Rome to the end times. This kind of "prophetic skip" is consistent with much of Old Testament prophecy. That is, many Old Testament prophecies describe, in great detail, events fulfilled up to and during the first coming of Christ, but then skip over the intervening ages all the way to the end times (see Isaiah 9:6-7; Zechariah 9:9-11).

Future Phases of the Roman Empire

It appears that this future, revived Roman Empire will go through three major stages. First, the G-10 will appear. This will mark the first phase of the revival of the Roman Empire and the initial stage of the one-world economic system. Second, a strong man, the future Antichrist, will emerge. He will consolidate these ten leaders and the people they represent into a united empire and probably extend its borders in various directions. The G-10, recognizing his stunning ability, will elect him to power by common consent (Revelation 17:13). He will take the G-10 to a whole new level of global influence. Third, there is the final stage of the revived Roman Empire when, by declaration or edict, its political and economic power extends to the entire earth. We'll discuss this third stage of the reunited Roman Empire in more detail in chapter 8.

It's probable that the revived Roman Empire will include nations from Europe and possibly even from northern Africa and some nations from western Asia, since the revived Roman Empire to some extent is viewed as including the three preceding empires that were largely Asiatic. As the Holy Land is the center of biblical interest, it would only be natural for the empire to include this area—especially when one considers that the Holy Land will evidently come under the influence of the Roman Empire as a result of the treaty with Israel mentioned in Daniel 9:27 and the warfare that will take place later in this area (Ezekiel 38–39; Daniel 11:40-45; Zechariah 14:1-3).

Although the specific identity of the ten kings, or world leaders, can't be determined at this time, there has been much speculation concerning the materials that form the toes of the image described in Daniel 2. The toes are said to be partly of iron and partly of pottery or dried clay. In the prophecy, attention is called to the fact that iron does not mix with the clay. Therefore, the feet of the image are the weakest portion of the entire structure. According to Daniel 2:41-43,

> The feet and toes you saw were a combination of iron
> and baked clay, showing that this kingdom will be

divided. Like iron mixed with clay, it will have some of the strength of iron. But while some parts of it will be as strong as iron, other parts will be as weak as clay. This mixture of iron and clay also shows that these kingdoms will try to strengthen themselves by forming alliances with each other through intermarriage. But they will not hold together, just as iron and clay do not mix (NLT).

It is clear that because the legs of iron represent the strength of the ancient Roman Empire, the clay in the feet and toes must in some sense denote the idea of political weakness or instability. The best interpretation is that the clay mixed with iron represents the diverse racial, religious, or political elements that are included in the confines of this final revived Roman Empire that contribute to its ultimate downfall. This view is supported by the fact that the revived Roman Empire, when it does reach its world stage, immediately begins to encounter difficulties that result in the final world conflict, which will be underway when Christ returns. Commentator Leon Wood supports this perspective:

> The reference may be either to intermingling strong people from strong countries to weaker people from weaker countries, or else strong people within a country with weaker people of that country, to provide greater overall strength...The effort at gaining overall strength in this way will fail. As baked clay and iron will not mix, so also these diverse elements will not mix. This means that the empire...will have its internal problems making for weakness.[1]

This mention of iron and clay, or inherent strength and weakness at the same time, is reflected in the European Union (EU) today. The EU has great economic and political clout, but its diversity in culture, language, and politics is also ever-present. Many interpreters of Bible prophecy have felt that the European Union will be a fulfillment of Daniel's predicted alignment of nations. One can easily see how the EU could become the feet and toes of iron and clay.

Before we leave our discussion of the ten toes and ten horns in Daniel, let me emphasize a point that's easy to forget when we get enmeshed in the details of biblical prophecy: Our quest for prophetic insight must never cause us to become unbalanced in our spiritual lives. Bible prophecy was given by God to bring change to our lives in the present, not so we could just cram our minds with secrets about the future. Let me repeat some challenging words from my friend Randall Price as a helpful reminder and practical application for our lives:

> What good is it to be able to understand the seven heads of Revelation 13:1 if we don't use our own head? Of what profit is it to discern the ten toes of Daniel 2:42-44; 7:24 if we don't move our own two feet? And what value is it to know about the great mouth that speaks lies (Daniel 7:8; Revelation 13:5), unless we open our own mouth and speak the truth?[2]

May the Lord never allow us to fall into the snare of merely knowing the truths about the end times and the Lord's coming yet fail to allow these truths to take hold of us.

E-Unification of the Roman Empire

Whether the European Union is the preliminary form of the G-10 group or it is the forerunner of another coalition or union of nations is impossible to predict with certainty. The final power bloc initially led by the Group of Ten will constitute the revived Roman Empire, which will possess the economic and political power necessary to control the Mediterranean. The supreme leader who emerges onto the world scene at that time must eventually be able to seize control of three of the G-10 leaders and create a consolidation of power very much like the Roman Empire of the past (Daniel 7:8).

It appears that the revived Roman Empire described by Daniel is beginning to take shape. The reunification of the Roman Empire began officially in 1957 with a treaty appropriately named The Treaty (or Treaties) of Rome. This treaty was signed on March 25, 1957, on Capitoline Hill, which is one of the famous Seven Hills of Rome. Gradually yet steadily since then, the nations of Europe have come together one by one.

The addition of ten new nations to the EU in 2007 brought the total number of member nations to 27. The addition of these nations expands the population of the EU to about half a billion people, making the EU surpass North America as the world's biggest economic zone. Of the ten nations officially admitted in 2004, eight are former Communist states from Eastern Europe, and two are Mediterranean islands.

Economic self-interest, national security, and the threat of international terrorism in Europe and the Middle East point to the necessity for an alliance of nations to help bring peace and economic prosperity to the region. The changes that are necessary for the EU to conform to the prophetic scenario in Daniel could take place rapidly in today's world.

Back Together Again

The Roman Empire ceased to exist almost 1600 years ago. The stage being set for its reunion, as predicted in the Bible, could be happening right before our eyes. The EU today has a 732-member parliament, a parliament building in Strasbourg, France, a presidency that rotates among the member nations every six months, a supreme court, a passport, and numerous committees. The EU also has one unified currency, the euro, which has been approved and adopted by 16 of the 27 member nations and is presently in circulation. This means the euro is the currency now used by 325 million people.

The EU is now working toward having a unified military and criminal justice system. What has developed in Europe over the past 50 years looks strikingly similar to what the Bible predicts for the end times. The basic governmental and economic components and structural elements are in place for some kind of ten-ruler group or committee to come on the scene in the EU and ascend to power, and then for one man to assume the EU presidency and take over the entire alliance.

It seems very likely at this point that America will become more and more isolationist in the wake of its long, bloody conflicts in Iraq and Afghanistan. When these wars finally grind to a halt, the United States will likely be reticent to involve itself militarily in any other nations for a long time unless it is attacked. As happened in the years immediately after the Vietnam War, America may turn within to address its own mounting problems at home. This withdrawal of U.S. forces from the world arena may be another factor that prepares the way for Europe to rise more quickly to assert itself in the world, especially in the Middle East.

While the EU as it stands now does not fulfill Bible prophecy, the events taking place in Europe today seem to be bringing together the reunited Roman Empire prophesied by Daniel over 2500 years ago. The stage is being set for a new alignment of power that will promise peace and economic stability to a world disrupted by catastrophe and on the brink of complete chaos. Yet, little will the world know that the seemingly beneficial G-10 will be the first tragic step in a series of events that will plunge the world into its darkest hour.

Runaway Inflation Rocks the World

The Sound of Approaching Hoofbeats

"With John, I have heard the distant sound of hoofbeats. I have seen the evil riders on the horizon of our lives…there is serious trouble ahead for our world, for all of us who live in it, and in the four horsemen of the Apocalypse there is both a warning and wisdom for those troubled days ahead."

Billy Graham
Author, *Approaching Hoofbeats*

Hyperinflation is one of those scary-sounding economic words. It just *sounds* bad. And it is. It can sweep a nation like a brush fire consuming everything in its path. By the time it's finally brought under control, the charred landscape is almost unrecognizable. The most famous hyperinflation in history occurred in the Weimar Republic (Germany) in 1923, topping out at a whopping 29,525 percent a month with prices doubling every 3.7 days. Here's a sobering description of what happened:

> Before World War I Germany was a prosperous country, with a gold-backed currency, expanding industry, and world leadership in optics, chemicals, and machinery. The German Mark, the British shilling, the French franc, and the Italian lira all had about equal value, and all were exchanged four or five to the dollar. That was in 1914. In 1923, at the most fevered moment of the German hyperinflation, the exchange rate between the dollar and the Mark was one trillion Marks to one dollar, and a wheelbarrow full of money would not even buy a newspaper. Most Germans were taken by surprise by the financial tornado...So the printing presses ran, and once they began to run, they were hard to stop. The price increases began to be dizzying. Menus in cafes could not be revised quickly enough. A student at Freiburg University ordered a cup of coffee at a cafe. The price on the menu was 5,000 Marks. He had two cups. When the bill came, it was for 14,000 Marks. 'If you want to save money,' he was told, 'and you want two cups of coffee, you should order them both at the same time.'...When the 1,000-billion Mark note came out, few bothered to collect the change when they spent it. By November 1923, with one dollar equal to one trillion Marks, the breakdown was complete. The currency had lost meaning.[1]

But as bad as the economy was in Germany in the early 1920s, it wasn't even close to what has happened in the African nation of Zimbabwe. In late 2008 and early 2009, inflation levels in Zimbabwe were spiraling out of control at 13.2 billion percent a month. Yes, that's billion with a *b*. Economists calculated the annual rate at a mind-numbing 516 quintillion. To put this in perspective, that's 516 followed by 18 zeros. People couldn't even afford to pay a cab fare. Money became meaningless.[2]

In December 2008, Zimbabwe began to circulate $200 million notes, just days after introducing the $100 million bill. After the $100 million notes began circulating, the price of a loaf of bread skyrocketed from 2 million to 35 million Zimbabwean dollars.[3] That was followed by the release of the $10 billion note, which was enough to buy two loaves of bread. After that came the $20 billion note, and then the $50 billion note in early January 2009, which, at the time, was just enough to buy two loaves of bread. With prices doubling every day, by the end of January, Zimbabwe was issuing $10 trillion, $20 trillion, and $50 trillion notes, and then finally $100 trillion notes, which were worth only $33 on the black market.

That's what runaway hyperinflation can do. And the Bible predicts that in the end times, hyperinflation will occur on a worldwide scale. Sometime after the G-10 comes together and the world begins to experience peace and safety (1 Thessalonians 5:1-3), the world economy will plummet into a black hole, triggering a global financial catastrophe. I believe this economic disaster will set the stage for the final global economic order and the final world ruler. As the crisis deepens, people everywhere will be willing to do anything to save themselves and the lives of their families and stop the slide into the abyss. This end-time economic calamity is vividly depicted in Revelation 6.

Riders on the Storm

Revelation 6:1-8 describes what is commonly known as the "four horsemen of the apocalypse." These four horses and their riders represent the first four of the seven seal judgments in Revelation. The events associated with the horsemen parallel the events prophesied by Jesus in Matthew 24:4-8, in what is sometimes called the *mini-Apocalypse*.

Matthew 24:4-8	Revelation 6:1-8
False Christs	Rider on the white horse
Wars and rumors of wars	Rider on the red horse
Famine	Rider on the black horse
Plagues (parallel passage in Luke 21:11)	Rider on the pale horse

While all four horses and their riders portend trouble on the horizon, the black horse gives us a very important clue about the kinds of conditions in the end times that will pave the way for the one-world, end-time economy of the Antichrist.

The Black Horse of Financial Collapse

In the Museum of Modern Art in New York City, Umberto Boccioni's *The City Rises* portrays the four horsemen of the Apocalypse in a modern, urban setting. The oil painting occupies a massive six-foot-six by nine-foot-ten canvas. It singles out the horror of the third horse and its rider. Boccioni depicts the black horse as a tornado spinning wildly above the other horsemen.[4] What an apt depiction! The black horse will whirl forth, leaving widespread destruction in its wake. Having lived in central Oklahoma for over 40 years, I know something about the devastation tornadoes can wreak. I live in "tornado alley." Boccioni had it right—the black stallion and its rider portend terrible ruin for the world.

As the third seal is broken in Revelation 6:5-6, the jet-black horse gallops across the globe in the horrific wake of the first two horsemen. The apostle John recorded what he saw:

> I looked, and behold, a black horse; and he who sat on it had a pair of scales in his hand. And I heard something like a voice in the center of the four living creatures saying, "A quart of wheat for a denarius, and three quarts of barley for a denarius, and do not damage the oil and the wine."

The third horse is black as midnight, black as tar. The mere color itself signals something ominous, dark, and dreadful. But what do the horse and rider represent? Although several different suggestions have been offered, it is clear they personify famine and hunger. And the black undoubtedly signifies the lamentation and sorrow that comes with extreme deprivation.

Four points favor this identification of the black horse and its rider. First, after the red horse and the outbreak of war, food shortages cannot be far behind. This is the way it has always been: Hunger is one of the wretched results of war.

Second, as we've already seen, the identification is confirmed by the parallel with Jesus' list of end-time signs in Matthew 24:5-7. According to Jesus, the first three birth pangs of the end times will be false messiahs, war, and famine. This runs parallel to the horsemen in Revelation 6:1-8.

Third, the color black often signifies the haunting specter of hunger. For instance, Lamentations 4:8-9 says, "Their appearance is blacker than soot, they are not recognized in the streets; their skin is shriveled on their bones. It is withered, it has become like wood. Better are those slain with the sword than those slain with hunger; for they pine away, being stricken for lack of the fruits of the field."

Fourth (and this is the clincher) is the fact that the rider holds a pair of scales in his hand. This refers to either a beam with trays or pans at both ends, or a device with a weight at one end and a tray or pan suspended at the other.[5] In Revelation 6:6, the rider is carefully weighing food on the scales. This reveals that food is in short supply. For food to be consumed in carefully weighed out portions is a sign of famine (Ezekiel 4:16-17).

The haunting phantom of famine rides forth.

The Voice of God

While John is mesmerized by the black horse and rider, who had a pair of scales in his hand, he suddenly hears an unidentified voice coming from "the center of the four living creatures," saying, "A quart of wheat for a denarius, and three quarts of barley for a denarius; and do not damage the oil and the wine" (Revelation 6:6). This is unusual because it is the only time in the description of the four horsemen that a voice speaks, other than the living creature who announces the coming of each horse and rider. Who is doing the speaking?

Several different answers have been given. Some believe this is Jesus, the Lamb, speaking. After all, He is the one who opens the seals that bring forth the four horsemen. But it seems more reasonable to identify this voice with God the Father, who is seated on His throne and surrounded by the four living creatures (Revelation 4:6-8). If this is correct, then God, enthroned in majesty and splendor, is breaking into the narrative to add His sovereign commentary on the severity of the coming judgment. This cry of the Almighty from His throne makes the warning of a coming world famine even more ominous. The black rider is very black indeed.

Famine in the Land

I don't know if you've ever been hungry before. I mean *really* hungry—to the point of experiencing a deep gnawing in the pit of your stomach. Or to the point you would eat about anything you could get your hands on.

For four years, I worked for Judge Hez Bussey on the Oklahoma Court of Criminal Appeals. He survived the Bataan Death March in the Philippines in 1942 and three-and-a-half years in Japanese concentration camps. When the Japanese surrendered in 1945, the judge, who was about five feet and ten inches tall, weighed a mere 103 pounds. He said if the war had lasted a few more weeks, he would not have survived. He used to tell me stories about eating bugs, worms, or anything he could get his hands on. He told me once about a group of hungry prisoners on a work detail leaping on a snake in the water and carving it up into pieces in a matter of seconds. His fingernails were disfigured from having bamboo shoots jammed underneath them during a Japanese interrogation concerning some stolen rice. He and a few other men had stolen the rice at the risk of their lives, but they didn't give in to the interrogators, even under merciless torture.

The average American knows nothing about going hungry. I know I don't. My idea of a fast is the time between lunch and dinner. Sadly, we have the opposite problem in our country—I read recently that 65 percent of Americans are overweight. About one in three is obese—that is, at least 100 pounds over their ideal body weight. We live in the land of plenty, and we should be deeply thankful for this tremendous blessing from God. But let's face it—too many of us spend way too much time in the pantry and refrigerator. We eat for entertainment and fun. There's an abundance of scrumptious food all around us.

According to the Bible, however, it's not always going to be this way. The black horse of famine is on the horizon. Before his ride is complete, the whole world will be like one giant concentration camp, and people will be desperate to find a morsel of food to bring momentary relief. How bad will it be? Revelation 6:6 gives us a glimpse at just two of the devastating consequences of this famine.

1. Terrible Inflation

The dire conditions of the future Tribulation period will be triggered by a financial meltdown. This economic tidal wave will result in runaway inflation, which will, in turn, trigger massive shortages. This will bring on a famine, and people will need a denarius to buy a measure of wheat or three measures of barley. A denarius in that day was a silver coin equal to an average day's wages for a working man. A measure or "quart" of grain in the first century was equal to slightly less than our modern-day quart. And one measure or quart of wheat was the basic portion of food for one person for one day. What this indicates is that the purchasing power of a denarius will drop far below what is normal. In other words, the world will experience runaway inflation, just like the Weimar Republic in the 1920s and Zimbabwe today. Food prices will be so high that it will take everything a person can earn just to buy enough food for one meal for an average person. The food prices listed in Revelation 6:6 are about eight to sixteen times higher than they were at the time John wrote the warning.

As prophecy scholar John Walvoord wrote: "To put it in ordinary language, the situation would be such that one would have to spend a day's wages for a loaf of bread with no money left to buy anything else. The symbolism therefore indicates a time of economic devastation and famine when life will be reduced to the barest necessities."[6]

2. Degenerating Quality of Food

With the world economy suffering runaway inflation, the kind of food people can afford will quickly degenerate. Because one day's wages will only buy enough food for one person per day, people will have to resort to lower-quality food just to put enough on the table for their families.

Wheat was the main food of the ancient world. Barley was a lesser-quality grain with less nutritional value, often used to feed animals. During the famine of the end times, people will quit buying their usual foods and will turn to cheaper foods. By eating food of grossly inferior quality, a family of three could eat three meals a day of barley, whereas they could eat only one meal of wheat.

To put this in terms of today's marketplace, it will take all the money a man or woman can earn in a day just to buy meat and potatoes for one person for one day, *or* macaroni and cheese or beans to feed a whole family for a day. The world will be consumed by the rider on the black horse; earth will writhe in the clutches of stabbing hunger.

Lifestyles of the Rich and Famous

Revelation 6:6 makes clear that the economic collapse and famine that breaks out during the first half of the Tribulation will not be universal. One group of people will be exempt from this horror. As the masses endure runaway inflation and lower-quality food, the superwealthy will enjoy a temporary reprieve from this time of judgment. At the end of verse 6 we read, "Do not damage the oil and the wine." This means that while the basic staples of life are being decimated, the oil and wine will go untouched. And in John's day, oil and wine were more in the categories of luxury than wheat and barley.[7]

During the coming Tribulation, the gulf between rich and poor will grow wider than ever before. Food will be so expensive that only the very wealthy will have enough. Famine will relentlessly hammer the middle and lower classes until the middle class disappears. The vast majority of people will wallow in misery, but the rich will continue to bask in the comforts of their luxurious lifestyle. The world will be radically divided among the elite "haves" and the mass of the "have-nots." The wealthy will continue to flourish. They will not only have the necessities of life, but will still enjoy the luxuries as well. This will make the suffering of the have-nots even more unbearable as they watch the privileged few indulge themselves in the lap of luxury.

I don't know about you, but to me this looks unfair. Why will the rich be exempt from God's judgment? Is God playing favorites? Not at all. The rich will escape this first wave of judgment, but as the Tribulation moves along, they too will cry out in despair. The rich will not escape God's judgment for long. When the sixth seal judgment is unleashed in Revelation 6:15-16, the wealthy will suffer the heavy hand of God's wrath.

> The kings of the earth and the great men and the commanders and the rich and the strong and every slave and free man hid themselves in the caves and among the rocks of the mountains; and they said to the mountains and to the rocks, "Fall on us and hide us from the presence of Him who sits on the throne, and from the wrath of the Lamb; for the great day of their wrath has come, and who is able to stand?"

The old poem by Friedrich von Logau (1604–1655) will be amply fulfilled…

> Though the mills of God grind slowly,
> Yet they grind exceeding small;
> Though with patience He stands waiting,
> With exactness grinds He all.

The Final New World Order

Economic upheaval always opens the door for massive change. Political opportunists take full advantage of desperate times to seize power and implement their vision. This was true in the past, is true today, and will still hold true in the future. This coming worldwide economic disaster will no doubt be a key part of the matrix of events that sets the stage for the one-world economy of the Antichrist. Just as with Hitler's rise to power, runaway inflation will pave the way for the Antichrist and his one-world, cashless economy. History will repeat itself. People desperate for the basic necessities of life will yearn for someone—anyone—who can provide real answers and solutions. They will gladly dispense with the delay of democratic processes and the normal channels of government. They will accept anyone who can stop the misery.

ONE WORLD UNDER ANTICHRIST

"I Am God and the World Is Mine"

*"We do not want another committee; we have too
many already. What we want is a man of sufficient
stature to hold the allegiance of all the people and
to lift us up out of the economic morass into which
we are sinking. Send us such a man, and whether
he be God or devil, we will receive him."*

PAUL HENRI SPAAK
First president of the United Nations
General Assembly and a key planner in
the formation of the European Economic
Community in 1957

The world today is looking for a leader. With mounting danger,
surging uncertainty, and escalating economic instability,
people everywhere are hungry for leadership and direction unlike
any time in human history. The problems we face are gloomy,

global, and growing. Everyone knows it. And everyone knows we need someone to give hope and chart a clear course for solving the world's mounting crises. Arnold Toynbee wisely noted, "The nations are ready to give the kingdoms of the world to any one man who will offer us a solution to our world's problems."[1] In *Forbes* magazine, Paul Johnson, an eminent British historian, said, "There's one lesson to be learned above all others: There is no substitute for prudent, strong and courageous leadership. This is what the civilized world currently lacks and must find—soon."[2]

The Bible predicts that just such a leader is coming.

He may already be here.

Satan's Main Man

Other than Jesus Christ, the main person in Bible prophecy and all of human history is the coming world ruler or Antichrist. My friend Dr. Harold Willmington aptly describes the uniqueness of this future world dictator:

> Since the days of Adam, it has been estimated that approximately 40 billion human beings have been born upon our earth. Four and one-half billion of this number are alive today. However, by any standard of measurement one might employ, the greatest human (apart from the Son of God himself) in matters of ability and achievement is yet to make his appearance upon our planet.[3]

Who is this satanic superman who has yet to burst on the world scene? What will he do? What will he be like? Where will he come from? Will he appear in our lifetime? Few people probably realize that there are more than 100 passages of Scripture that describe the origin, nationality, character, career, kingdom, and final doom of the Antichrist. God doesn't want us to be preoccupied with this individual in an unhealthy, unbalanced way, but clearly God wants us to know some things about this coming prince of darkness. While the focus of this book is the global economic system the Antichrist will establish in the end times, we'll find it helpful to gain a more complete understanding of this world ruler—who he is, and what he will do. Let's spend some time getting acquainted with what the Bible reveals about this mysterious figure.

AKA (Also Known As)

Without any doubt, the most commonly used and most familiar title for the sinister, end-time world ruler is Antichrist. But this is not his only designation in the Bible. Just as Christ is known by different names and titles throughout Scripture, the one who will come to imitate and oppose Him is also known by various designations.

A.W. Pink, the great theologian, notes, "Across the varied scenes depicted by prophecy there falls the shadow of a figure at once commanding and ominous. Under many different names, like the aliases of a criminal, his character and movements are set before us."[4]

Here are the top ten titles for the coming Antichrist:

1. The little horn (Daniel 7:8)

2. A king, "insolent and skilled in intrigue" (Daniel 8:23)

3. The "prince who is to come" (Daniel 9:26)

4. The one "who makes desolate" (Daniel 9:27)

5. The king who "will do as he pleases" (Daniel 11:36)

6. A foolish shepherd (Zechariah 11:15)

7. The man of lawlessness (2 Thessalonians 2:3)

8. The son of destruction (2 Thessalonians 2:3)

9. The rider on the white horse (Revelation 6:2)

10. The beast who comes up out of the sea (Revelation 13:1-9; 17:3,8)

Profiling the Coming World Ruler

Revelation 12 is a key chapter in the unfolding drama of the end times. It's a highly symbolic chapter that graphically portrays the characters and events of the last days. It has been said that Revelation 12 is the most symbolic chapter in the most symbolic book in the Bible. In this chapter, Satan is depicted as a great red dragon who is cast out of heaven as the result of a great cosmic war. Revelation 12 ends by noting that "the dragon was enraged" and then Revelation 13 begins, "The dragon [Satan] stood on the sand of the seashore. Then I saw a beast coming up out of the sea."

The scene here is dramatic. Satan, the enraged dragon, is standing on the seashore—probably a reference to the Mediterranean Sea—calling the "beast" or Antichrist forth from the sea of the nations so he can embody the beast and bring his program for world dominion into full swing. Revelation 13 describes the coming world ruler in great detail. Much of what is revealed about the Antichrist in Revelation chapters 13 and 17 builds upon and amplifies what the prophet Daniel wrote in the Old Testament. Let's put Daniel and Revelation together and develop a character profile of what this final world ruler will be like:

1. An Intellectual Genius (Daniel 8:23)

The Antichrist will overwhelm and captivate the world with his superhuman intellect and powers of perception. Obviously, anyone who can hold the entire world under his spell and quickly convince the G-10 to give him complete control must have intellectual abilities that far exceed those of normal men.

2. An Oratorical Genius (Daniel 7:8,11; 11:36; Revelation 13:5)

The whole world will be swayed by the hypnotic spell of the Antichrist's words. Over and over again the Bible mentions his great speaking ability. When he talks, everyone else will listen. As A.W. Pink wrote,

> So it will be with this daring counterfeiter: he will have a mouth speaking very great things. He will have a perfect command and flow of language. His oratory will not only gain attention but respect. Rev. 13:2 declares that his mouth is "as the mouth of a lion" which is a symbolic expression telling of the majesty and awe-producing effects of his voice. The voice of a lion excels that of any other beast. So the Antichrist will outrival orators ancient and modern.[5]

3. A Political Genius (Daniel 9:27; Revelation 17:11-12)

The Antichrist will emerge from relative obscurity to take the world political scene by storm. He won't attract much attention when he first enters the political arena. He will begin without any fanfare as a "little" horn among the ten horns in a reunited Roman Empire. Then he will quickly rise among the ranks and be elected by the G-10 to rule over the reunited Roman Empire (Revelation 17:13). He will be the consummate unifier and diplomat.

At first, everyone will love the Antichrist. He will assume power under the stealth of diplomacy. His platform will be peace and prosperity. Emerging with an olive branch in his hand, he will weld opposing forces together with ease. All the dreams of the United Nations will be realized in his political policies. He will even temporarily solve the Middle Eastern political situation, which may well earn him accolades such as the Nobel Peace Prize. Daniel 9:27 reveals he will bring such peace to the Middle East that the Temple Mount area in Jerusalem will be returned to Jewish sovereignty. He will undoubtedly be hailed as the greatest peacemaker the world has ever seen.

4. An Economic Genius (Daniel 11:43; Revelation 13:16-17)

The Antichrist will be the CEO of the world's economy. He will set interest rates, prices, stock values, and supply levels. Under his leadership, everything will be nationalized under his personal control. From the midpoint of the Tribulation until the second coming of Christ, no one will be able to buy or sell without his permission. People all over the world will be compelled to take his mark. His one-world economy will be run by his sidekick, the false prophet (we'll meet him in the next chapter).

5. A Military Genius (Revelation 6:2; 13:2)

At the midpoint of the Tribulation the mask will come off and the beast will replace the olive branch with a sword. He will subjugate the whole world. All the greatness of Alexander and Napoleon will be as nothing compared to him. No one will be able to stand in the way of his conquest. He will crush everything and everyone before him. He will be the final great Caesar over the ultimate form of the Roman Empire.

6. A Religious Genius (2 Thessalonians 2:4; Revelation 13:8)

Satan's prodigy will be able to do what no other religious leader has ever done. He will do what neither Mohammed, nor Buddha, nor any pope has ever been able to do: unite the world in worship. All the religions of the world will be brought together in the worship of one man. Just think what genius and power and deception it will take to pull this off! Preparation for the acceptance of worshipping a man is well under way. The world, like never before, is looking for a great world leader, a messiah, a savior to solve the profound predicaments the world faces today. The world is well down the road toward worshipping the ultimate idol.

To help us better envision what the Antichrist will be like, H.L. Willmington has provided this helpful analogy with American presidents. The coming world ruler will possess:

> The leadership of a Washington and Lincoln
>
> The eloquence of a Franklin Roosevelt
>
> The charm of a Teddy Roosevelt
>
> The charisma of a Kennedy
>
> The popularity of an Ike
>
> The political savvy of a Johnson
>
> The intellect of a Jefferson[6]

antichrists and Antichrist

The term "antichrist" (Greek, *antichristos*) is found only five times in the New Testament, all in the epistles of John (1 John 2:18,22; 4:3; 2 John 7):

> Children, it is the last hour; and just as you heard that antichrist is coming, even now many antichrists have

> appeared; from this we know that it is the last hour (1 John 2:18).

> Who is the liar but the one who denies that Jesus is the Christ? This is the antichrist, the one who denies the Father and the Son (1 John 2:22).

> Every spirit that does not confess Jesus is not from God; and this is the spirit of the antichrist, of which you have heard that it is coming, and now it is already in the world (1 John 4:3).

> Many deceivers have gone out into the world, those who do not acknowledge Jesus Christ as coming in the flesh. This is the deceiver and the antichrist (2 John 7).

According to 1 John 2:18, John's readers knew about the predicted advent of the Antichrist. They had heard that "Antichrist is coming." The title "antichrist" might have been new, but the idea was not. John had undoubtedly personally taught his audience about the Antichrist, and they had certainly read about the Antichrist's coming in Old Testament books such as Daniel. Years earlier, when Paul was in Ephesus, he had taught these same believers what John was now addressing in his letters. And Paul also taught the Thessalonian believers about this final great deceiver (2 Thessalonians 2:1-12).[7]

John's purpose was to warn his fellow believers about false teachers who came in the spirit of Antichrist, displaying hostility toward the true Christ. John was concerned about the doctrinal error of denying the person of Jesus Christ. He stated that even in his own day many "antichrists" (false teachers) had arisen who were denying the true Christ and deceiving many. The emphasis in John's epistles is on the doctrinal error taught in his own day. However, the antichrists in John's day were only the initial stage of the antichrist philosophy of Satan that was already at work (2 Thessalonians 2:7; 1 John 4:3).

Notice in 1 John 2:18 that John refers to antichrist (*antichristos,* singular), who is coming in the future, and antichrists (*antichristoi,* plural) who are already present.[8] John's use of the singular form for "the Antichrist" in stark contrast to the plural "antichrists" clearly denotes that the earlier mention referred to a single individual. In using both the singular and the plural forms, John was teaching that the antichrists of his day, who were false teachers, embodied the denying, deceiving spirit of the future Antichrist. They were forerunners of the Antichrist, and they were powerful evidence that his spirit was already at work in the world.[9]

James Montgomery Boice is representative of this almost universal view: "[John] is saying that the spirit that will characterize the final antichrist is already working in those who have recently left his readers' congregations. The future antichrist will be a substitute for Christ, as much like Jesus as possible for a tool of Satan to be."[10]

The renowned scholar F.F. Bruce agrees. "So it was with John. That Antichrist would come he and his readers knew, and in the false teachers he discerned the agents, or at least the forerunners, of Antichrist, sharing his nature so completely that they could be called 'many antichrists.'"[11]

In other words, John looked beyond the many antichrists of his own day to the one ultimate Antichrist, who will culminate the manifestation of the lawless system that denies Christ and deceives men.

Christ versus the Antichrist

Before we go any further in this discussion of Antichrist, it's important that we pause briefly to make sure we know who we are talking about. The prefix *anti* can mean "against"/"opposed to" or "instead of"/"in place of." This raises an important issue: Will this future Antichrist be "against" Christ, or "in place of" Christ? That is, does *anti* refer to opposition or an exchange? Will he be a false, counterfeit Messiah, or will he simply work against Christ Himself?

Both of these meanings are undoubtedly included in the term *Anti*christ. He will be the archenemy and the ultimate opponent of the Lord Jesus. The origin, nature, and purpose of Christ and Antichrist are diametrically opposed. This list of titles and characteristics reveals the gaping chasm between Christ and His adversary.[12]

Christ	Antichrist
The Truth	The Lie
The Holy One	The Lawless One
The Man of Sorrows	The Man of Sin
The Son of God	The Son of Destruction
The Mystery of Godliness	The Mystery of Iniquity
The Lamb	The Beast
Cleanses the Temple	Desecrates the Temple

The total opposition of Antichrist to Christ is seen in the following contrasts.[13]

Feature	Christ	Antichrist
Origin:	Heaven	Bottomless pit
Nature:	The Good Shepherd	The foolish shepherd
Destiny:	To be exalted on high	To be cast down into hell
Goal:	To do His Father's will	To do his own will
Purpose:	To save the lost	To destroy the holy people

Authority:	His Father's name	His own name
Attitude:	Humbled Himself	Exalts himself
Fruit:	The True Vine	The vine of the Earth
Response:	Despised	Admired

In every area that could be imagined, Christ and Antichrist are fundamentally opposed.

The Antichrist will be anti (against) Christ. The Antichrist will not only be anti Christ—that is, against Christ—but he will also be anti Christ in the sense of "in place of" Christ. He will be an amazing parody or counterfeit of the true Christ. He will be a substitute Christ, a mock Christ, a pseudo Christ, an imitation Christ. In John 5:43, Jesus said, "I have come in My Father's name, and you do not receive Me; if another comes in his own name, you will receive him." The one coming in his own name will be the world's final false Messiah, the Antichrist. He will attempt to be the "alter ego" of the true Christ.

As has often been pointed out, Satan has never originated anything except sin. He has always counterfeited the works of God. Antichrist is no exception. He is Satan's ultimate masterpiece—a false Christ and forged replica of Jesus, the true Christ and Son of God.

Here are 20 ways Antichrist will mimic the ministry of the true Son of God:

Christ	Antichrist
Miracles, signs, and wonders (Matthew 9:32-33; Mark 6:2)	Miracles, signs, and wonders (Matthew 24:24; 2 Thessalonians 2:9)
Appears in the millennial temple (Ezekiel 43:6-7)	Sits in the Tribulation temple (2 Thessalonians 2:4)

Is God (John 1:1-2; 10:36-38)	Claims to be God (2 Thessalonians 2:4)
Is the Lion from Judah (Revelation 5:5)	Has a mouth like a lion (Revelation 13:2)
Makes a peace covenant with Israel (Ezekiel 37:26)	Makes a peace covenant with Israel (Daniel 9:27)
Causes men to worship God (Revelation 1:6)	Causes men to worship Satan (Revelation 13:3-4)
Followers sealed on their forehead (Revelation 7:4; 14:1)	Followers sealed on their forehead or right hand (Revelation 13:16-18)
Worthy name (Revelation 19:16)	Blasphemous names (Revelation 13:1)
Married to a virtuous bride (Revelation 19:7-10)	Married to a vile prostitute (Revelation 17:3-5)
Crowned with many crowns (Revelation 19:12)	Crowned with ten crowns (Revelation 13:1)
Is *the* King of kings (Revelation 19:16)	Is called "the king" (Daniel 11:36)
Sits on a throne (Revelation 3:21; 12:5; 20:11)	Sits on a throne (Revelation 13:2; 16:10)
Sharp sword from his mouth (Revelation 19:15)	Bow in his hand (Revelation 6:2)
Rides a white horse (Revelation 19:11)	Rides a white horse (Revelation 6:2)
Has an army (Revelation 19:14)	Has an army (Revelation 6:2; 19:19)
Violent death (Revelation 5:6; 13:8)	Violent death (Revelation 13:3)
Resurrection (Matthew 28:6)	Resurrection (Revelation 13:3,14)
Second coming (Revelation 19:11-21)	Second coming (Revelation 17:8)
1000-year worldwide kingdom (Revelation 20:1-6)	3½-year worldwide kingdom (Revelation 13:5-8)
Part of a holy Trinity (Father, Son and Holy Spirit) (2 Corinthians 13:14)	Part of an unholy trinity (Satan, Antichrist, and False Prophet) (Revelation 13)

J. Dwight Pentecost aptly summarizes the meaning of the word *Antichrist:* "Satan is seeking to give the world a ruler in place of Christ who will also be in opposition to Christ so that he can rule over the world, instead of Christ."[14]

The Cashless System of Revelation 13

One of the key components of the Antichrist's reign will be his world economic system. Revelation 13:16-18 is the biblical entry point for any discussion of the coming one-world economy and the coming cashless society.

> He causes all, the small and the great, and the rich and the poor, and the free men and the slaves, to be given a mark on their right hand or on their forehead, and he provides that no one should be able to buy or to sell, except the one who has the mark, either the name of the beast or the number of his name. Here is wisdom. Let him who has understanding calculate the number of the beast, for the number is that of a man; and his number is six hundred and sixty-six.

The Antichrist may move the world to a global currency to facilitate his economic system, or it may have already been set up long before he comes on the scene. While a one-world currency might seem impossible, remember that 16 nations in Europe now share one currency—the euro. Many are beginning to ask, "Why can't 192 nations share the same currency?" Because the economic aspect of Antichrist's reign is the main focus of this book, chapter 10 is devoted entirely to the economic system the Antichrist will create and his famous mark—666.

Could the Antichrist Be a Muslim?

There are a growing number of prophecy teachers and authors who are claiming that the coming Antichrist or world ruler will be a Muslim. Some speculate that he will be the manifestation of the Islamic messiah (Mahdi). They generally reject the idea of a reunited Roman Empire centered in Europe as the dominant force in the end times. For them, world power is dominated by a Muslim caliphate and ruled over by the Islamic messiah.

This identification is based on several points. First, they often point to the basic fact that Islam is the fastest-growing religion in the world, including in the United States, Canada, and Europe, and that in a very short time it will pass Christianity as the world's largest religion. From this they argue that it simply makes sense that the world's final military, political, and spiritual leader will be from this soon-majority religion.

Second, adherents of this view sometimes note that the vast majority of the nations that are listed in the Bible as key end-time players are currently Islamic nations. The geographical locations mentioned in Scripture include what are now Syria, Jordan, Egypt, Sudan, Libya, Lebanon, Turkey, and Iran. Since these are the key end-time nations, they argue that it makes most sense if the coming world ruler is a Muslim from one of these nations. They also usually hold that Gog, in Ezekiel 38–39, the leader of an end-time invasion against Israel, is the same person as the Antichrist.

Third, proponents of this view point to the many similarities between the Muslim Mahdi or messiah and the biblical Antichrist. A number of similarities are cited—for example, both will be world rulers, both will be global spiritual leaders, both will make seven-year treaties, and both will ride on a white horse.[15]

These similarities are cited as proof that these two end-time figures are the same person.

Fourth, the Bible says that the Antichrist will be a terrible persecutor of the Jewish people. Those who hold to the Islamic Antichrist position note that the Mahdi will launch a targeted campaign against Jews and Christians, and will attack Israel. They interpret 2 Thessalonians 2:4 as saying he will establish the seat of his authority on the Temple Mount. Because the Temple Mount is under Muslim control, they believe it makes more sense for the Antichrist to be an Islamic figure.

Fifth, some highlight the fact that the Antichrist will use beheading as a form of execution against those who reject his rule (Revelation 20:4). They hasten to point out that this is a favorite means of execution among followers of Islam.

But does the Islamic Antichrist view have support in the Bible?

The only passage of Scripture I know of that gives insight into the religious background of the Antichrist is found in Daniel 11:36-39. Describing the final world ruler as "the king who does as he pleases," Daniel said,

> He will exalt and magnify himself above every god…He will show no regard for the gods of his fathers or for the desire of women, nor will he show regard for any other god; for he will magnify himself above them all. But instead he will honor a god of fortresses, a god whom his fathers did not know; he will honor him with gold, silver, costly stones and treasures. He will take action against the strongest of fortresses with the help of a foreign god.

While I would agree that there are some interesting parallels between the biblical Antichrist and the Islamic Mahdi, for me,

Daniel 11:36-39 precludes the Islamic Antichrist view. Daniel said the Antichrist will exalt himself "above every god" and "will honor…a god whom his fathers did not know." The Antichrist could be someone who was a Muslim at some point in his life, but the Bible makes it clear that by the time he comes to power he will have rejected Allah and turned to another god—the god of fortresses or military might, and ultimately, himself. So, if he is a Muslim at some point in his life, which is possible, this passage makes clear that when he comes to power, he will have turned his back on all religion and established himself as god.

Second Thessalonians 2:4 states that the Antichrist will take his seat in the temple of God, which is a reference to a rebuilt or third Jewish temple in Jerusalem (the second temple was destroyed in A.D. 70), and will declare that he is god. No practicing Muslim could ever do this. Doing so would violate the central tenet of Islam that there is one God, who is Allah. If the Antichrist declared himself God, he would no longer be a follower of Islam.

For these reasons, I don't hold to the Islamic Antichrist view. I believe the Bible teaches that he will be a God-hating, Christ-rejecting megalomaniac who will despise every religion and every god other than himself and his ultimate master, Satan.

Top Ten Keys to Antichrist's Identity

1. He will not be recognized until after the rapture of believers to heaven.

2. He will have obscure beginnings and then rise to world prominence as a man of peace.

3. He will be a Gentile world leader from the geographical area of the former Roman Empire.

4. He will rule over the reunited Roman Empire (the "Unholy" Roman Empire).

5. He will make a seven-year peace covenant with Israel.

6. He will be assassinated and come back to life.

7. He will break his treaty with Israel at the midpoint of the Tribulation and invade the land.

8. He will sit in the temple of God and declare himself to be God.

9. He will desecrate the temple in Jerusalem by having an image of himself placed in it.

10. He will rule the world politically, economically, and religiously for 3½ years.

Could the Antichrist Come from the United States?

According to Scripture, the coming Antichrist will be a Gentile who will rule the entire world for three-and-a-half years. Because America is the most powerful nation in the world, people often ask if the Antichrist could come from the United States, or even if he could be a U.S. president because the president of the United States is considered by many to be the most powerful individual on earth.

Daniel 9:26 tells us that the Antichrist ("the prince who is to come") will be of the same nationality as the people who destroyed the second Jewish temple in A.D. 70. Of course, we know that the Romans destroyed the temple. This indicates that the Antichrist will be of Roman origin. This doesn't mean necessarily that he will be Italian, but simply that he will rise from within the reunited Roman Empire.

Interestingly, the 1976 movie *The Omen* begins with the birth of the Antichrist in a dimly lit hospital in Rome. A chilling poem from this same movie also makes reference to the belief that the coming Antichrist will arise from the Holy Roman Empire.

As we look at our world today, the Holy Roman Empire is indeed rising before our eyes in the European Community. The rise of Antichrist may not be far behind!

The Antichrist will arise out of the reunited Roman Empire. This limits his place of origin to Europe, the Middle East, or North Africa. Most people have taken this to mean that he will come out of one of the nations of Europe that formed the nucleus of the old Roman Empire, or that he might even come from Rome itself.

There are some who say that because the United States was begun by people from European nations that constituted the Roman Empire, and because elements of its language and laws are derived from Rome, perhaps it is possible that the Antichrist could come from America. They even wonder if he could be an American president. But I don't think so. It seems best to hold that the Antichrist will come out of Europe, which has its roots in the Roman Empire that existed in John's day when he prophesied about the Antichrist in Revelation.

However, regardless of where the Antichrist comes from, one thing is sure: He is coming. And he will do exactly what the Bible predicts.

The Antichrist's Activities

1. He will appear in "the time of the end" of Israel's history (Daniel 8:17).
2. His manifestation will signal the beginning of the day of the Lord (2 Thessalonians 2:1-3).

3. His manifestation is currently being hindered by the one "who now restrains" (2 Thessalonians 2:3-7).

4. His rise to power will come through peace programs (Revelation 6:2). He will make a covenant of peace with Israel (Daniel 9:27). This event will signal the beginning of the seven-year Tribulation. He will later break that covenant at its midpoint.

5. Near the middle of the Tribulation, the Antichrist will be assassinated or violently killed (Daniel 11:45; Revelation 13:3,12,14).

6. He will descend into the abyss (Revelation 17:8).

7. He will be raised back to life (Revelation 11:7; 13:3,12,14; 17:8).

8. The whole world will be amazed and follow after him (Revelation 13:3).

9. He will be totally controlled and energized by Satan (Revelation 13:2-5).

10. He will subdue three of the ten kings in the reunited Roman Empire (Daniel 7:24).

11. The ten kings will give all authority to the beast (Revelation 17:12-13).

12. He will invade the land of Israel and desecrate the rebuilt temple (Daniel 9:27; 11:41; 12:11; Matthew 24:15; Revelation 11:2).

13. He will mercilessly pursue and persecute all believers and especially the Jewish people (Daniel 7:21,25; Revelation 12:6).

14. He will set himself up in the temple as God (2 Thessalonians 2:4).

15. He will be worshipped as God for three-and-a-half years (Revelation 13:4-8).

    His claim to deity will be accompanied by great signs and wonders (2 Thessalonians 2:9-12).

16. He will speak great blasphemies against God (Daniel 7:8; Revelation 13:6).

17. He will rule the world politically, religiously, and economically for three-and-a-half years (Revelation 13:4-8,16-18).

18. He will be promoted by a second beast, who will lead the world in worship of the beast (Revelation 13:11-18).

19. He will require all to receive his mark (666) to buy and sell (Revelation 13:16-18).

20. He will establish his political and economic capital in Babylon (Revelation 17).

21. He and the ten kings will destroy Babylon (Revelation 18:16-19).

22. He will kill the two witnesses (Revelation 11:7).

23. He will gather all the nations against Jerusalem (Zechariah 12:1-2; 14:1-3; Revelation 16:16; 19:19).

24. He will fight against Christ when He returns to earth and suffer total defeat (Revelation 19:19-21).

25. He will be cast alive into the lake of fire (Daniel 7:11; Revelation 19:20).

Is the Antichrist Alive Today?

Amazingly, in a 1999 *Newsweek* poll, 19 percent of Americans said that they believe the Antichrist is alive on earth now.

That's one in five Americans who believe that the Antichrist is alive right now. And in the same poll, nearly half of those who accept biblical prophecy believe he is alive now.[16] Could they be right? Let's find out what the Bible has to say.

As we consider this poll's results, I want to make three key points. First, I want to make it crystal clear that I don't believe anyone can say for sure that the Antichrist is alive today. I believe, based on 2 Thessalonians 2:3-7, that the Antichrist will not be revealed until after believers have been raptured to glory. So it is a waste of time to try to figure out if some particular person in Washington, London, Paris, or Rome is the Antichrist. The Bible never specifically identifies the Antichrist by name and never tells us to figure out who he is. The number 666, the number of his name, will not become discernible until after the rapture. According to the Scripture, he will be revealed *after* the rapture of the church and the removal of the restraining power of the Holy Spirit (2 Thessalonians 2:3-7). He will emerge on the world scene when he makes his peace covenant with Israel (Daniel 9:27). That will be his formal introduction to the world, and that takes place *after* God's people are in heaven.

Second, while no one knows if *the* Antichrist is alive today, we can be certain that *an* antichrist is alive in the world at this very moment. Writing late in the first century A.D., the apostle John said that "the spirit of the antichrist" was already at work undermining and opposing the work of God (1 John 4:3; see also 2:18). We can be certain that the *spirit* of antichrist is alive and well today! The apostle Paul also said that in his day, Satan was already at work trying to bring the Antichrist onto the world scene (2 Thessalonians 2:6-7).

I believe that Satan has a man ready in every generation, a satanically prepared vessel to take center stage and rule the world.

After all, this is Satan's goal (Isaiah 14:12-14). God has stated that He will rule the world through His Son, the Christ, so Satan's goal is to usurp God and rule the world through his man, the Antichrist. Because Satan doesn't know when Christ will come to establish His kingdom, he is prepared in every generation with his man to try to take over the world and to stand against Christ and the establishment of his glorious kingdom. A quick overview of history affirms this.

In the years after the flood, Satan ruled the world of that day through a mighty leader named Nimrod (Genesis 10:8-12; 11:1-9). In the early days of Israel's history, Satan ruled a large part of the then-known world through Pharaoh. Later, in about 600 B.C., came the mighty Babylonian monarch Nebuchadnezzar (Daniel 1–4). Then came possibly the greatest ruler of them all, Alexander the Great (Daniel 8:5-8; 11:2-4). Satan persecuted Israel mercilessly through a Syrian king named Antiochus Epiphanes in about 165 B.C. Satan made his greatest strides to world domination through the Roman Caesars. He tried again through Napoleon. Then Hitler. Then Stalin. And I firmly believe that Satan has someone alive today who could set up a rival kingdom to usurp the rightful place of the King of kings if the situation presents itself. There is always *an* antichrist ready, prepared by Satan. I believe Satan has someone ready right now, somewhere unknown to us. But he cannot bring his program on the scene because the restraining power of the Holy Spirit is holding him back. Yet in God's timing, when the restrainer is taken out of the way, Satan will finally be allowed to bring his long-awaited agenda into full swing (2 Thessalonians 2:6-7).

Third, while I want to re-emphasize that I can't say for sure whether *the* Antichrist is alive today, I wouldn't be surprised if he is. Many of the key pieces to the prophetic puzzle seem to be

coming together. We have the United States of Europe forming before our eyes in the European Union. Globalism is here
along with the advanced technology that makes possible a one-
world government and economy. The world is ripe for a great
peacemaker, especially one who can bring peace to the Middle
East.

No one can say for sure that the Antichrist is alive right now.
But if Jesus happens to return within the next 40-50 years, that
requires the Antichrist to almost certainly be alive right now.
Of course, the Bible never tells us how old Antichrist will be
when he comes on the world scene. And, I am not saying that
Jesus *is* coming in the next 40–50 years, because no one knows
the time of His coming. All we can say is that His return in the
next few decades seems highly probable. If this is true, then the
Antichrist is probably alive somewhere on the Earth today. He
may even be on the world political scene, waiting in the wings
for his moment.

Prophecy teacher Gary Frazier paints this chilling picture:

> Somewhere at this moment there may be a young man
> growing to maturity. He is in all likelihood a brooding,
> thoughtful young man. Inside his heart, however, there
> is hellish rage. It boils like a cauldron of molten lead.
> He hates God. He despises Jesus Christ. He detests the
> Church. In his mind there is taking shape the form of
> a dream of conquest. He will disingenuously present
> himself as a friend of Christ and the Church. Yet…
> He will, once empowered, pour out hell itself onto
> this world. Can the world produce such a prodigy?
> Hitler was once a little boy. Stalin was a lad. Nero was
> a child. The tenderness of childhood will be shaped
> by the devil into the terror of the *antichrist*.[17]

All the clues seem to point in the same direction. The emergence of Antichrist could be very soon. And that means the coming of the Lord is even closer.

Are you ready to meet Him at His coming?

God's Got It All Under Control

The possibility that the Antichrist and his coming kingdom and world economic system may arise soon can be frightening to many people. As Daniel and the book of Revelation reveal, the beast is the epitome of evil. He will be indwelled and controlled by Satan himself. In Revelation 13, we dare not miss a little four-word phrase that appears six times—"was given to him."

Revelation 13:5a	"there *was given to him* a mouth speaking arrogant words"
Revelation 13:5b	"authority to act for forty-two months *was given to him*"
Revelation 13:7a	"It *was also given to him* to make war with the saints"
Revelation 13:7b	"authority over every tribe and people and tongue and nation *was given to him*"
Revelation 13:14	"the signs which it *was given him* to perform"
Revelation 13:15	"It *was given to him* to give breath to the image of the beast"

Antichrist and his henchman the false prophet (whom we will meet in the next chapter) do nothing on their own. Everything is under the control of God's sovereign hand—their actions, words, duration, and miracles. As powerful as the Antichrist is, his power will be a limited, delegated power. Just as in the Old Testament book of Job, Satan and his pawn, the Antichrist, will be able to do only the things that God allows. The Antichrist will wreak havoc in the world, but it's comforting to know that God is in control even during Earth's darkest hour and that no one and nothing can exceed the boundaries God has set in His own wisdom.

Accept Christ Now!

I'll never forget seeing the movie *The Omen* for the first time in 1976 when I was in high school (a remake was produced in 2006). While the movie is a fictional horror film, its warning is very real—the Antichrist is coming, and he may even be alive and walking the Earth right now.

There is a gripping scene early in the movie *The Omen*. On the morning after the nightmarish fifth birthday party for Damien (the Antichrist), a Catholic priest named father Brennan pays an unannounced visit to Ambassador Thorn's office. As soon as father Brennan is alone with Thorn (Damien's father), he blurts out a startling warning to the ambassador: "You must accept Christ as your Savior. You must accept Him, now!"

Ambassasor Thorn is stunned as the priest proceeds to tell him that his young son is really the son of Satan—the Antichrist. Thorn is incensed and calls for security guards to haul the priest away. Father Brennan's warning to accept Christ is considered foolish by Thorn. Interestingly, however, even when Thorn finally realizes Damien is the Antichrist, he still refuses to accept Christ. The same warning is still applicable to unbelievers today: "You must accept Christ as your Savior. You must accept Him, now!"

Scripture teaches that when the Antichrist appears, most people will refuse to accept Christ and will instead turn to follow the lawless one.

Second Thessalonians 2:8-12 says,

> Then that lawless one will be revealed whom the Lord will slay with the breath of His mouth and bring to an end by the appearance of His coming; that is, the one whose coming is in accord with the activity of Satan, with all power and signs and false wonders, and with all the deception of wickedness for those who perish, because they did not receive the love of the truth so as to be saved. For this reason God will send upon them a deluding influence so that they will believe what is false, in order that they all may be judged who did not believe the truth but took pleasure in wickedness.

If you are not a Christian, don't assume time is on your side and you can wait and receive Christ later. No one knows when he or she might die, and we certainly don't know when the rapture will occur. Don't put it off any longer: Accept Jesus Christ as your Savior now!

The Bible tells us that when Jesus Christ died on the cross He purchased a full pardon from the penalty of sin for you and me. The pardon has been bought and paid for, and God offers it to every person. All we have to do to make this pardon effective in our lives is simply to receive it, to accept it (John 1:12).

Why not do it now? (For more on this, see the section titled "The Final Invitation" on page 182.)

THE COMING WORLD COMMERCE SECRETARY

End-Time Economic Czar

> *"I saw another beast coming up out of the earth; and he had two horns like a lamb and he spoke as a dragon...He performs great signs...And he deceives those who dwell on the earth...and he provides that no one will be able to buy or sell, except the one who has the mark."*
>
> REVELATION 13:11,13-14,17

Two of the greatest forces in the world are religion and money. It's probably safe to say that more blood has been spilled, more energy has been expended, and more passion has been devoted to these things than almost everything else combined. Religion and money can motivate people to do extraordinary things, or cause them to sink to the depths of their depravity. They shape the destinies of peoples and nations. Brought together in the hands of self-seeking opportunists, they form the most explosive combination on planet Earth. And according to the end-time template presented in Scripture, both will have a prominent role in what is to come. A global, blasphemous, deceptive religion will be joined with a one-world economy to form the most powerful religo-economic machine in history.

The False "Profit"

There have always been false prophets and false teachers. One of Satan's chief methods of operation is to counterfeit and corrupt the true message of God through his false messengers. And Satan will dramatically increase the number of messengers in the end times. The Bible says that in the last days of planet Earth there will be many false prophets who will perform great signs and wonders and spew out deceiving lies (Matthew 24:24).

From this mass of deception one false prophet will rise high above all the rest in his ability to capture the world's attention. He is called "the false prophet" in Revelation 16:13, 19:20 and 20:10, and is also known as the second beast in Revelation 13:11-18. The false prophet will use his power to do great signs and wonders to convince the world to follow the Antichrist. The false prophet is the final person in the unholy trinity of the end times (see Revelation 16:13; 19:20–20:2; 20:10). Satan is a counterfeit Father; the Antichrist is a counterfeit Son; the false prophet is the satanic counterfeit of the Holy Spirit, or what we could call the "Antispirit."

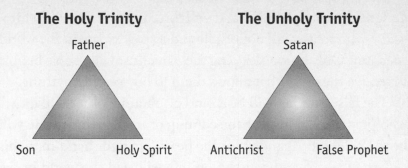

The Holy Trinity

Father

Son   Holy Spirit

The Unholy Trinity

Satan

Antichrist   False Prophet

Just as the ministry of the Holy Spirit is to give glory to Christ and convict men to trust and worship Him, the chief ministry of the false prophet will be to glorify the Antichrist and lead people to trust and worship him. Here are five key ways the false prophet will counterfeit the ministry of the Holy Spirit:

Holy Spirit	False Prophet
Points men to Christ	Points men to Antichrist
Instrument of divine revelation	Instrument of satanic revelation
Seals believers to God	Marks unbelievers with the number of Antichrist
Builds the body of Christ	Builds the empire of Antichrist
Enlightens men with the truth	Deceives men by miracles

The Antichrist, or first beast (Revelation 13:1-10) will primarily be a military and political figure; whereas the second beast (Revelation 13:11-18) will be a religious and economic figure. Using a fatal mixture of hellish religion and economic control, he will institute and administer the most sinister system one could ever imagine. In the end times, there will be no separation of church and state. The church will be the state, as the world ruler will declare himself to be God and will force people to worship him. Those who refuse will not be allowed to participate in the world economy. Only by worshipping the Antichrist will people be able to receive the mark that allows them to buy or sell anything.

The false prophet will be a kind of "satanic John the Baptist" who prepares the way for the coming of the Antichrist. He will be the chief propagandist for the beast, his right-hand man, his closest colleague and companion. He will lead the world in the false worship of its end-time emperor.

The Antichrist and the false prophet are mentioned together four places in the New Testament:

Revelation 13:1-18	they share a common goal
Revelation 16:13	they share a common agenda for the world
Revelation 19:20	they share a common sentence
Revelation 20:10	they share a common destiny

There are three key things about the false prophet that are emphasized in Revelation 13:11-18: his deceptive appearance, his devilish authority, and his deadly activity.

His Deceptive Appearance (Revelation 13:11)

Revelation 13:11 provides a description of the second end-time beast: "I saw another beast coming up out of the earth; and he had two horns like a lamb and he spoke as a dragon." Evidently the false prophet will be a master of deception. He is described as a wild beast, a lamb, and dragon. No greater contradiction could be imagined.

He has the nature of a wild beast.	He is hostile to God's flock. He ravages God's people.
He has the appearance of a lamb.	He looks gentle, tender, and harmless.
He has the voice of a dragon.	He is the voice of hell itself belching forth the fiery lies of Satan. When he speaks, he becomes Satan's mouthpiece.

John Phillips summarizes the deceptive appearance and deadly approach of the False Prophet:

> The role of the false prophet will be to make the new religion appealing and palatable to men. No doubt it will combine all the features of the religious systems of men, will appeal to man's total personality, and will take full advantage of his carnal appetite. The dynamic appeal of the false prophet will lie in his skill in combining political expediency with religious passion, self-interest with benevolent philanthropy, lofty sentiment with blatant sophistry, moral platitude with unbridled self-indulgence. His arguments will be subtle, convincing, and appealing. His oratory will be hypnotic, for he will be able to move the masses to tears or whip them into a frenzy. He will control the communication media of the world and will skillfully organize mass publicity to promote his ends. He will be the master of every promotional device and public relations gimmick. He will manage the truth with guile beyond words, bending it, twisting it, and distorting it. Public opinion will be his to command. He will mold world thought and shape human opinion like so much potter's clay. His deadly appeal will lie in the fact that what he says will sound so right, so

sensible, so exactly what unregenerate men have always wanted to hear.[1]

His Devilish Authority (Revelation 13:12)

Revelation 13:12 tells us the second beast "exercises all the authority of the first beast in his presence. And he makes the earth and those who dwell in it to worship the first beast, whose fatal wound was healed." The second beast will "exercise all the authority of the first beast"—that is, he will have great authority delegated to him by the Antichrist. The false prophet's mission will be to use every means given to him by the Antichrist to cause everyone on earth to worship the Antichrist. He will carry out the plans and wishes of the Antichrist and lead the worldwide cult of Antichrist worship. He will be also empowered by the same source as the first beast—Satan himself. Like Joseph Goebbels with Hitler, he will be inspired by the same authority and share the same diabolical agenda as the Antichrist.

His Deadly Activity (Revelation 13:13-18)

Revelation 13:13-18 delineates seven deadly activities on the part of the false prophet. These activities reveal how he will use his influence and experience during the days of the Great Tribulation to bring the entire world under the control of one religion and one economy.

1. He will come up out of the Earth (13:11)

Many students of Bible prophecy have taken this to mean that the false prophet will be a Jew. The first beast, or Antichrist, comes up out of the sea, which may indicate he is a Gentile from among the sea of nations (Revelation 17:15). The second beast, or false prophet, comes up out of the Earth or land, which could refer to Israel. However, it makes more sense to see the false prophet as a Gentile, just like the first beast. He will help the first beast persecute the Jewish people, so it is doubtful he is Jewish. His coming up out of the earth is meant to contrast him with the Holy Spirit, who comes down from heaven. The false prophet is "earthly" in the fullest sense of the word.

2. He will bring down fire from heaven and perform other miracles (13:13-14)

We have to remember that not all miracles are from God. The second beast will do the same miracle Elijah did in the Old Testament to prove that the Lord is the true God by calling down fire from heaven. The deception of the end times will be unlike anything the world has ever seen. In Matthew 24:24-25, Jesus said, "False Christs and false prophets will arise and will show great signs and wonders, so as to mislead, if possible, even the elect. Behold, I have told you in advance." The undue focus of many people today, even within professing Christianity, on great signs and wonders could be unknowingly paving the way for the rise of the false prophet.

3. He will mimic the miracle of the two witnesses, just like Egyptian magicians counterfeited the miracles of Moses (Exodus 7:11-13, 22; 8:7; Revelation 11:4-6)

Just as Satan will have his two men in the end times, the beast and the false prophet, so the Lord will have His two men in the end times to witness for Him in Earth's darkest days. These men, called the two witnesses, are described in Revelation 11:3-11. They will do great signs and wonders. The false prophet will do his miracles as a direct challenge to them, just like the Egyptian magicians did with Moses and Aaron.

4. He will erect an image of the Antichrist for all the world to worship (13:14)

At the midpoint of the coming Tribulation, the Antichrist will defile the rebuilt Jewish temple in Jerusalem and declare himself to be God (2 Thessalonians 2:4). The Bible refers to this as the "abomination of desolation" (Matthew 24:15). Because the Antichrist won't be able to stay in the temple all the time, the false prophet will construct an image of him that will be placed in the holy of holies in the temple. This is the second stage or phase of the abomination of desolation. As with the great golden image of King Nebuchadnezzar on the plain of Dura in Daniel 3, all people will have to bow to this image or die suddenly by execution or slowly by starvation (because they won't have access to food, which cannot be bought without the mark of the beast).

5. He will raise the Antichrist from the dead (13:14)

While this is not stated explicitly in the text, it is strongly implied. The death and resurrection of the Antichrist is mentioned three times in Revelation 13 (verses 3,12,14). Because the false prophet is a miracle worker who deceives the world, it is probable that Satan will use the false prophet as his human instrument to raise the Antichrist back to life. The world, which rejected the true resurrected Christ, will follow after the false Christ in amazement after he comes back to life. For more details about this, see the section at the end of the book titled, "Some Questions You Might Be Asking."

6. He will give life to the image of the beast (13:15)

The image that is erected in the beast's honor won't be like any other image ever created. Like something out of science fiction or a horror film, it will be animated. It will speak and breathe. Satan's deception will reach its zenith under the final world ruler and his passionate promoter.

7. He will control world commerce on behalf of the beast, forcing everyone to take the mark of the beast (13:16)

The crowning achievement for the second beast will be the implementation of a global registration of all people. He will use a totally controlled economy to secure the rule of the first beast, the Antichrist. No one will be able to buy or sell without pledging allegiance to the beast, receiving his mark, and submitting to the global registration system. His economic program is set forth in Revelation 13:16-17: "He causes all, the small and the great, and the rich and the poor, and the free men and the slaves, to be given a mark on their right hand or on their forehead, and he provides that no one will be able to buy or to sell, except the one who has the mark, either the name of the beast or the number of his name." Notice the universal scope of his control. It extends to "all." He will exercise iron-fisted control over the basic fundamentals of supply (no one will be able to sell) and demand (no one will be able to buy).

No one will be able to go to the mall, eat at a restaurant, fill a gas tank, pay utility bills, buy groceries, pay to get the lawn mowed, or make a mortgage payment without the mark of the beast—the Tribulation trademark. We will discuss this end-time economic system in greater detail in chapter 10 when we consider the meaning of the mark of the beast.

The Shadow of His Coming

A global economy is coming. For it to come to fruition, there will have to be some kind of global government under centralized control. The Bible predicts that an end-time finance secretary will serve as an absolute czar over the global economy and world religion. On behalf of the Antichrist and his blasphemous religion, the false prophet will exercise complete control of supply and demand. Under his guidance, the final world economic system will become reality. We don't exactly know how it will be implemented, or when it will be in place, but it does appear that the preparations are in full swing for its rise.

We can see its shadow appearing even now.

10

BABYLON, THE GREAT CITY

Wall Street of the End Times

> *"Geography is destiny."*
> NAPOLEON BONAPARTE

> *"In that day Babylon will dominate and rule the world. The capital of Antichrist will be Babylon, and he will have the first total dictatorship...In that day everything will center in Babylon. The stock market will be read from Babylon—not New York. Babylon, instead of Paris will set the styles for the world. A play, to be successful, will have to be a success in Babylon, not London."*
> J. VERNON MCGEE

A one-world economic system is coming. We see it in the Bible and in today's headlines. But where will this financial system be located? What will be its capital city? The Bible tells us that when the final commercial system is unveiled, it won't be in New York, London, Paris, or Shanghai. It will be in Babylon. According to the Bible, as the end of the age draws near, the focus of the world will be drawn back to the place where it all began, the city of Babylon, in modern Iraq. To understand how this will happen and why, we need to go all the way back to the beginning. Back to the first unified rebellion against God. Back to Babel.

Babylon in the Beginning

After the worldwide flood recorded in Genesis 7–8, as the planet became repopulated, the human race was all gathered in one place. According to Genesis 10–11, Nimrod was the human tyrant or dictator who led the entire global community. These first globalists shook their collective fist in God's face and defied His command to scatter over the face of the earth (Genesis 9:1). They all settled in the land of Shinar at Babel and decided to build a city and a tower to signify and promote their unity.

The city represented their governmental, political unity, and the tower or ziggurat they wanted to build would symbolize their religious unity. This ziggurat that reached high into the sky was no doubt intended to be a place of occult worship of the stars and heavens. Therefore, the first federation or "united nations" was a society built to bring the human race together to exclude God and exalt man, to deify man and dethrone God. We could call the Tower of Babel the first "United Nations building."

All this played right into Satan's plan. While he is not mentioned by name in Genesis 10–11, we can be certain that the old serpent introduced in Genesis 3 was working feverishly to energize this rebellious plan. In such a situation, Satan could control, influence, and direct world affairs through one man. And he could be "god" in the eyes of all men through occult worship and practices. After all, that is Satan's ultimate desire—to usurp God. Moreover, evil could spread through the whole race with ease because everyone was in one place speaking one language. False religion could easily convert the masses with little to stand in its way.

Of course, God was in total control. He saw what puny man was doing, and He came down and confounded man's language, thus scattering man all over the face of the earth (Genesis 11:5-8). That was the official end of the first one-world government, religion, and economy. But Satan wasn't finished. He set out immediately to bring the world back together so he could control it all again.

Globalism Reverses Babel

Ever since that initial attempt at globalism, when Satan ruled the world through one man, Nimrod, it has been Satan's goal to get the world together again so he can rule it all. Just think about world history: It's the record of one person after another trying to rule the world. All of the power-hungry rulers who have cruelly subjugated nations under their feet have been energized by Satan to foster this great goal of globalization.

Now, for the first time in history since Genesis 11 and the Tower of Babel, globalization is within man's (and Satan's) reach. Globalization is much more appealing to people today in the post-9/11 world than it was before. All the necessary elements are in place for full-blown, all-out globalization: the Internet, travel to almost any place on the planet in a matter of hours, rapid communications, incredible means of surveillance, satellites, weapons of mass destruction that can be used as threats to control others, intertwined world economic markets, the World Bank, and more.

Satan almost has the world back to Babel. All he needs now is to bring one man onto the world stage who can take over everything—another Nimrod to rule the world as his puppet. It could happen soon. The advancements over the last few decades have made globalism possible for the first time since Genesis 10–11. We must remember that the global world of Antichrist cannot occur in a vacuum. Preparations must help pave the way. Current events all around us are moving the world closer and closer to the edge.

Writing back in 1965, Billy Graham recognized how world conditions were leading us toward Antichrist's global empire:

> There are so many interesting references in the Bible to a future world government ruled by a great Antichrist…It is obvious that the world's acceptance of one-man rule must be preceded by a period of preparation. At a recent peace conference in Washington, speaker after speaker referred to the necessity and possibility of a world government. In the Gideon Seymour Memorial Lecture at the University of Minnesota, Arnold Toynbee said: "Living together as a single family is the only future mankind can have now that Western technology has simultaneously annihilated distance and invented the atomic bomb." He added: "The alternative to the destruction of the human race is a worldwide social fusion of all the tribes, nations, civilizations, and religions of man."[1]

Make no mistake. Globalism is here to stay and will steadily increase as world organizations take more and more control over national and local governments and individual lives. Modern technology will enable globalists to gain control over government and especially the economy. It's much easier to create a one-world economy than a one-world government. But if one can gain control over the world's purse strings, then political control won't be far behind. What we see today strikingly portends the global economy of the end times that Antichrist will use to leverage total control over everything for the last three-and-a-half years of this age.

Babylon in the Apocalypse

The book of Revelation contains 404 verses, and 42 of those verses deal with Babylon (Revelation 17–18). When you add in Revelation 14:8 and 16:19, which speak of Babylon's future, the total number of verses dealing with Babylon goes up to 44. That's 11 percent of the entire book of Revelation devoted to one subject—Babylon.

Think about that: In the final book of the Bible, God's great apocalypse or unveiling of the future, one out of every nine verses concerns Babylon. Obviously, Babylon retains a key place in the mind of God and in His final plan for the ages.

For over 150 years, students of Bible prophecy have believed the final world ruler will establish a key headquarters or maybe even the world capital in the rebuilt city of Babylon in modern-day Iraq, just 50 miles south of Baghdad. This conclusion is based on prophecies found in Isaiah 13, Jeremiah 50–51, Zechariah 5:5-11, and Revelation 17–18.

Babylon: Biblical Wall Street

A few years ago it seemed rather far-fetched that the center of world power would go back to the Middle East. But since then we have experienced oil shortages, and when the supply of oil is cut off, the whole world feels it. In this way the nations of the Middle East wield tremendous power. Also, the wealth of the world is being transferred to the Middle East because of the price of oil. So it's no longer hard to imagine Babylon becoming the great commercial capital of the world as predicted in Revelation 18:

> After these things I saw another angel coming down from heaven, having great authority, and the earth was illumined with his glory. And he cried out with a mighty voice, saying, "Fallen, fallen is Babylon the great! She has become a dwelling place of demons and a prison of every unclean spirit, and a prison of every unclean and hateful bird. For all the nations have drunk of the wine of the passion of her immorality, and the kings of the earth have committed acts of immorality with her, and the merchants of the earth have become rich by the wealth of her sensuality."
>
> I heard another voice from heaven, saying, "Come out of her, my people, so that you will not participate in her sins and receive of her plagues; for her sins have piled up as high as heaven, and God has remembered her iniquities. Pay her back even as she has paid, and give back to her double according to her deeds; in the cup which she has mixed, mix twice as much for her. To the degree that she glorified herself and lived sensuously, to the same degree give her torment and mourning; for she says in her heart, 'I sit as a queen and I am not a widow, and will never see mourning.' For this reason in one day her plagues will come, pestilence and mourning and famine, and she will be burned up with fire; for the Lord God who judges her is strong.
>
> And the kings of the earth, who committed acts of immorality and lived sensuously with her, will weep and lament over her when they see the smoke of her burning, standing at a distance because of the fear of her torment, saying, 'Woe, woe, the great city, Babylon,

the strong city! For in one hour your judgment has come.'

And the merchants of the earth weep and mourn over her, because no one buys their cargoes any more—cargoes of gold and silver and precious stones and pearls and fine linen and purple and silk and scarlet, and every kind of citron wood and every article of ivory and every article made from very costly wood and bronze and iron and marble, and cinnamon and spice and incense and perfume and frankincense and wine and olive oil and fine flour and wheat and cattle and sheep, and cargoes of horses and chariots and slaves and human lives. The fruit you long for has gone from you, and all things that were luxurious and splendid have passed away from you and men will no longer find them. The merchants of these things, who became rich from her, will stand at a distance because of the fear of her torment, weeping and mourning, saying, 'Woe, woe, the great city, she who was clothed in fine linen and purple and scarlet, and adorned with gold and precious stones and pearls; for in one hour such great wealth has been laid waste!' And every shipmaster and every passenger and sailor, and as many as make their living by the sea, stood at a distance, and were crying out as they saw the smoke of her burning, saying, 'What city is like the great city?' And they threw dust on their heads and were crying out, weeping and mourning, saying, 'Woe, woe, the great city, in which all who had ships at sea became rich by her wealth, for in one hour she has been laid waste!' Rejoice over her, O heaven, and you saints and apostles and prophets, because God has pronounced judgment for you against her."

Then a strong angel took up a stone like a great

millstone and threw it into the sea, saying, "So will Babylon, the great city, be thrown down with violence, and will not be found any longer. And the sound of harpists and musicians and flute-players and trumpeters will not be heard in you any longer; and no craftsman of any craft will be found in you any longer; and the sound of a mill will not be heard in you any longer; and the light of a lamp will not shine in you any longer; and the voice of the bridegroom and bride will not be heard in you any longer; for your merchants were the great men of the earth, because all the nations were deceived by your sorcery. And in her was found the blood of prophets and of saints and of all who have been slain on the earth" (verses 1-24).

Revelation 17–18 tells us more about this great city of Babylon, providing six clues that help identify this city:

1. Babylon is a literal city (Revelation 17:18).

2. Babylon is a city of worldwide importance and influence, probably the capital city of the world in the end times (Revelation 17:15,18).

3. Babylon and the Antichrist are very closely connected with one another. The woman (Babylon) is pictured riding on the beast (Antichrist).

4. Babylon is not only the center of false religion in the end times but is the mother or fountainhead of all spiritual harlotry or false religion (Revelation 17:4-5; 18:1-2). Only one place in the Bible is mentioned as the source of all false religion— Babylon (Genesis 11).

5. Babylon is the center of world commerce

(Revelation 18:9-19). Under the Antichrist, religion and commerce will share the same geographical location. The future Babylon, just like its ancient predecessor in Genesis 11, will be both a city and a system.

6. At the end of the Tribulation, Babylon will be destroyed suddenly and completely, never to rise again (Revelation 18:8-10,21-24). The world economy will be completely dismantled in "one hour" (verse 17).

Together, these clues reveal that Babylon will be the great religious, economic capital of the Antichrist's kingdom in the last days. But what city is represented by Babylon?

Babylon Means Babylon

This great harlot city of the last days has been variously identified with the Roman Catholic Church and the Vatican, apostate Christendom, New York City, Jerusalem, and Rome. As you can see, there is hardly a consensus on the identity of Babylon. However, I believe the *best view* is that Babylon is the literal city of Babylon on the Euphrates in modern-day Iraq, which will be rebuilt in the last days. There are seven factors that favor this identification.

First, the great city that is described as the last days' capital of Antichrist is specifically called "Babylon" six times (Revelation 14:8; 16:19; 17:5; 18:2,10,21). While it is possible that the name Babylon is a code name for Rome, New York, Jerusalem or some other city, there is no indication in the text that the name is to be taken figuratively or symbolically. Thus it is best to understand it as referring to literal Babylon. Henry Morris supports this literal understanding: "It must be stressed again that *Revelation* means 'unveiling,' not 'veiling.' In the absence of any statement in the context to the contrary, therefore, we must assume that the term Babylon applies to the real city of Babylon, although it also may extend far beyond that to the whole system centered at Babylon as well."[2]

Second, Babylon is the most-mentioned city in the Bible other than Jerusalem. Babylon is referred to almost 300 times in Scripture. Babylon is also pictured as the epitome of evil and rebellion against God—it is Satan's capital city on earth.

1. Babylon is the city where man first began to worship himself in organized rebellion against God (Genesis 11:1-11).

2. Babylon was the capital city of the first world ruler, Nimrod (Genesis 10:8-10; 11:9).

3. Nebuchadnezzar, king of Babylon, destroyed the city of Jerusalem and the temple in 586 B.C.

4. Babylon was the capital city of the first of four Gentile world empires to rule over Jerusalem.

Since Babylon was the capital city of the first world ruler and is pictured as Satan's capital city on Earth throughout Scripture, it makes sense that in the end times, he will once again raise up this city as the capital city of the final world ruler. Charles Dyer, in his excellent book *The Rise of Babylon*, says, "Throughout history, Babylon has represented the height of rebellion and opposition to God's plans and purposes, so God allows Babylon to continue during the final days. It is almost as though he 'calls her out' for a final duel. But this time, the conflict between God and Babylon ends decisively. The city of Babylon will be destroyed."[3] Also,

Revelation 18:5 says of Babylon, "Her sins have piled up as high as heaven, and God has remembered her iniquities." The mention of sins piling up "as high as heaven" is a clear allusion back to Genesis 11:4, when the residents of Babylon built a "tower whose top will reach into heaven."

Third, the literal city of Babylon fits the criteria for the city described in Revelation 17–18. As New Testament scholar Robert Thomas notes, "Babylon on the Euphrates has a location that fits this description politically, geographically, and in all the qualities of accessibility, commercial facilities, remoteness of interferences of church and state, and yet centrality in regard to the trade of the whole world."[4] Henry Morris highlights the advantages of Babylon as a world capital:

> Babylon is indeed a prime prospect for rebuilding, entirely apart from any prophetic intimations. Its location is the most ideal in the world for any kind of international center. Not only is it in the beautiful and fertile Tigris-Euphrates plain, but it is near some of the world's richest oil reserves.
>
> Computer studies for the Institute of Creation Research have shown, for example, that Babylon is very near the geographical center of all the earth's land masses. It is within navigable distances to the Persian Gulf and is at the crossroads of the three great continents of Europe, Asia, and Africa.
>
> Thus there is no more ideal location anywhere for a world trade center, a world communications center, a world banking center, a world educational center, or especially, a world capital! The greatest historian of modern times, Arnold Toynbee, used to stress to all his readers and hearers that Babylon would be the

best place in the world to build a future world cultural metropolis.

With all these advantages, and with the head start
already made by the Iraqis, it is not far-fetched at all to
suggest that the future capital of the "United Nations
Kingdom," the ten-nation federation established at the
beginning of the Tribulation, should be established
there.[5]

Fourth, the Euphrates River is mentioned by name twice in
Revelation (9:14; 16:12). In Revelation 9:14, we read that four fallen
angels are being held at the Euphrates River awaiting the appointed
time for them to lead forth a host of demons to destroy one-third of
mankind. In Revelation 16:12, the sixth bowl judgment is poured
out and dries up the Euphrates River to prepare the way for the
kings of the East. These references to the Euphrates point to the
fact that something important and evil is occurring there. That
the rebuilt city of Babylon on the Euphrates will function as a
religious and economic center for Antichrist is a good explanation
for the mention of the Euphrates River in Revelation.

Fifth, Zechariah 5:5-11 records an incredible vision that per-
tains to the city of Babylon in the last days:

> The angel who was talking with me came forward and
> said, "Look up and see what's coming." "What is it?" I
> asked. He replied, "It is a basket for measuring grain,
> and it's filled with the sins of everyone throughout the
> land." Then the heavy lead cover was lifted off the basket,
> there was a woman sitting inside it. The angel said, "The
> woman's name is Wickedness," and he pushed her back
> into the basket and closed the heavy lid again. Then I
> looked up and saw two women flying toward us, gliding

on the wind. They had wings like a stork, and they picked up the basket and flew into the sky. "Where are they taking the basket?" I asked the angel. He replied, "To the land of Babylonia, where they will build a temple for the basket. And when the temple is ready, they will set the basket there on its pedestal" (NLT).

The prophet Zechariah, writing in about 520 B.C., 20 years after the fall of Babylon to the Medo-Persians, saw evil returning to its original place in Babylon in the future. In this vision Zechariah sees a woman whose name is "Wickedness." Then he sees this woman carried away in a basket, in the last days, to the land of Babylon, where a temple will be built for her.

The parallels between Zechariah 5:5-11 and Revelation 17–18 are striking:

Zechariah 5:5-11	Revelation 17–18
woman sitting in a basket	woman sitting on the beast, seven mountains, and many waters (17:3,9,15)
emphasis on commerce (a basket for measuring grain)	emphasis on commerce (merchant of grain 18:13)
woman's name is "Wickedness"	woman's name is "Babylon the Great, the Mother of all Harlots and of the Abominations of the Earth"
focus on false worship (a temple is built for the woman)	focus on false worship (18:1-3)
woman is taken to Babylon	woman is called Babylon

God's Word teaches that in the end times, wickedness will again rear its ugly head in the same place where it began—Babylon. Did you notice that in both Zechariah 5 and Revelation 17–18 Babylon is associated with false religion and world commerce?

John's prostitute will fulfill Zechariah 5 as Babylon is established in the last days as the city that embodies evil and houses the headquarters of the world economic system.

Sixth, the city of Babylon was never destroyed suddenly and completely as is predicted in Isaiah 13 and Jeremiah 50–51. Those prophecies, then, must refer to a future city of Babylon that will be totally destroyed in the Day of the Lord.

Seventh, Jeremiah 50–51 clearly describes the geographical city of Babylon on the Euphrates. The many parallels between Jeremiah 50–51 and the future Babylon in Revelation 17–18 indicate that both passages are describing the same city.

Parallels Between Jeremiah 50–51 and Revelation 17–18[6]		
	Jeremiah 50–51	Revelation 17–18
compared to a golden cup	51:7a	17:3-4 and 18:6
dwelling on many waters	51:13a	17:1
involved with nations	51:7b	17:2
named the same	50:1	18:10
destroyed suddenly	51:8a	18:8
destroyed by fire	51:30b	17:16
never to be inhabited	50:39	18:21
punished according to her works	50:29	18:6
fall illustrated	51:63-64	18:21
God's people flee	51:6,45	18:4
heaven to rejoice	51:48	18:20

The city of Babylon will be rebuilt in the last days to serve as the religious and commercial capital for the Antichrist's empire. Wickedness will return to this place for its final stand. Then, at the end of the Tribulation, in the seventh bowl judgment, God will put it in Antichrist's heart to fulfill His purpose by destroying the great city of Babylon with fire (17:16-17; 18:8). Babylon will fall, never to rise again!

The rise of Iraq in recent years on the world political and economic scene because of her huge revenues from oil is not an accident. In spite of the First Gulf War, the Iraq War, and a great deal of political upheaval, Iraq is a viable nation today. Iraq's prominent position on the world stage seems to be a key part of God's plan for the last days.

United States Helping Rebuild Babylon

The government of Iraq is moving forward with plans to protect the amazing archaeological remains of the ancient city of Babylon in preparation for building a modern city of Babylon. The project, originally begun by the late Saddam Hussein, is aimed eventually at attracting scores of "cultural tourists" from all over the world to see the splendor of Mesopotamia's most renowned city. What's more, the U.S. government is contributing $700,000 toward "The Future of Babylon" project through the budget of the State Department via the U.S. embassy in Baghdad. According to reports,

> Officials hope Babylon can be revived and made ready for a rich future of tourism, with help from experts at the World Monuments Fund (WMF) and the U.S. embassy. The Future of Babylon project launched last month seeks to "map the current conditions of Babylon and develop a master plan for its conservation, study and tourism."[7]

Mariam Omran Musa, head of a government inspection team based at the site, said, "We don't know how long it will take to reopen to tourists. It depends on funds. I hope that Babylon can be reborn in a better image."[8]

While this is just one small step, it reveals that the rebuilding of Babylon is on the radar. Yet many still wonder whether Babylon could really become a world economic center like the one depicted in Revelation 18. No one can predict exactly what might occur in the Middle East, but some of the current building projects being carried out by Iraq's neighbors could be faint foreshadows of the rise of Babylon.

Cities in the Sand

Saudi Arabia also has a bold initiative to build new cities in the desert. Six of these cities are planned, and four are being built simultaneously:

- Prince Abulaziz bin Mousaed Economic City
- Knowledge Economic City
- Japan Economic City
- King Abdullah Economic City

Two other economic cities are planned, but specific sites have not yet been selected. The King Abdullah Economic City, known as KAEC, is located on the Red Sea; it's the flagship project. *The New York Times* describes the construction of the city:

> Amid a forest of cranes, towers and beams rising from the desert, more than 38,000 workers from China, India, Turkey and beyond have been toiling for two years in unforgiving conditions—often in temperatures exceeding 100 degrees—to complete one of the world's largest petrochemical plants in record time.

By the end of the year, this massive city of steel at
the edge of the Red Sea will take its place as a cog of
globalization: plastics produced here will be used to
make televisions in Japan, cell phones in China and
thousands of other products to be sold in the United
States and Europe. Construction costs at the plant,
which spreads over eight square miles, have doubled
to $10 billion because of shortages in materials and
labor. The amount of steel being used is 10 times the
weight of the Eiffel Tower.[9]

It's the first time in decades that an entire city has been built
from scratch. And nothing like this has ever been done before in
modern times. The city that's rising out of the desert will ultimately
be about the size of Washington, D.C. and have a population of
about 1.5 million. The total project will take about 20 years to
complete, and the total cost is estimated at about $120 billion.
The first tenants have already begun to move in, and it's antici-
pated that by about 2012 "the trickle will turn into a flood."[10]

Of course, no one is saying that the current efforts in Babylon are anything even close to the scale of what's happening in
Saudi Arabia, but the main point is that if the oil-rich Saudis
can build huge economic centers in the desert, so can the Iraqis.
Experts say that Iraq has the second largest proven oil reserves in
the world, but some believe that Iraq may even have more than
Saudi Arabia. Due to Saddam Hussein's reign of terror, Iraq has
not been explored on a scale even close to that of its Persian Gulf
neighbors. To provide some perspective, Texas has about one million oil wells, while Iraq only has a little more than 2000.

Babylon sits right in the middle of the Persian Gulf area, where
about two-thirds of the world's proven oil reserves lie under the
golden sands. When Iraq gets fully stabilized and can begin taking

full advantage of its vast oil resources, it could easily rebuild Babylon as the crown jewel of the nation.

A city located in the center of the greatest oil reserves in the world would be a very attractive place for a world ruler to set up shop to control the world's energy supply and dominate the world economy.

The Final Piece Is Missing

Thus far we have identified the first stage of the coming world economy as the emergence of the G-10. We have also considered the global crisis that will precipitate the final world economic system, the man who will establish it, the man who will administer it, and the place where it will be centered. But there's still one more key piece missing from the puzzle—the indispensible piece that puts it all together, the linchpin of the financial system of the end times.

What is this missing key?

The mark of the beast.

666.

11

UNLOCKING THE MYSTERY OF THE MARK—666

"Will that be the right hand or the forehead?"

> *"It is very clear from studying Revelation 13, 17, and 18 that the Antichrist will have total control of the world's economy during the last three years of the Tribulation. His primary tool will be absolute domination of the money supply. And how will he accomplish this great feat? Through a famous means commonly known as 'the mark of the beast.'"*
>
> TIM LAHAYE AND JERRY B. JENKINS
> *Are We Living in the End Times?*

The church I have the privilege of pastoring is Faith Bible Church in Edmond, Oklahoma. When we were first establishing the street address at our current site, which spans tens acres, the postal service told us we could choose any number from 500 to 699 North Coltrane. One man in our church suggested that we select the number 666 North Coltrane as our church address because it would certainly get people's attention and be easy to remember. I have to admit that because I love Bible prophecy so much, this suggestion almost tempted me. However, my better judgment prevailed, and we settled for the more mundane 600 North Coltrane.

The number 666, the so-called mark of the beast, may be one of the most intriguing topics in all of Bible prophecy. There has probably been more speculation, sensationalism, and silliness over this topic than any other I can think of in Bible prophecy.

Revelation 13:16-18 is the biblical key that opens the door to the meaning of 666, the mark of the beast, the coming one-world economy and the coming cashless society:

> He causes all, the small and the great, and the rich and the poor, and the free men and the slaves, to be given a mark on their right hand or on their forehead, and he provides that no one will be able to buy or to sell, except the one who has the mark, either the name of the beast or the number of his name. Here is wisdom. Let him who has understanding calculate the number of the beast, for the number is that of a man; and his number is six hundred and sixty-six.

Let's consider what Scripture actually says about the mark of the beast and this universal economic system by answering eight important questions:

1. Is the mark of the beast past or future?

2. What is the mark of the beast?

3. What's the significance of 666?

4. Why 666?

5. What's the purpose of the mark?

6. What does the mark reveal about the Antichrist?

7. Does modern technology relate to the mark of the beast?

8. How will the Antichrist do it?

Is the Mark of the Beast Past or Future?

When we consider the mark of the beast, we must first determine the time period during which this mark is used. Has the mark of the beast already been fulfilled, or is it something that still lies in the future?

Those scholars who hold to a preterist (past) view of the book of Revelation maintain that the mark of the beast was completely fulfilled during the reign of the Roman ruler Nero (A.D. 54–68).[1] They argue that the Greek form of *Neron Caesar,* written in Hebrew characters, has a numerical value equivalent to 666. They further bolster their argument by pointing out that some ancient Greek manuscripts contain the variant number 616 instead of 666 and that the Latin form *Nero Caesar* is equivalent to 616.[2] Proponents of the preterist view also point to the fact that the persecution under Nero lasted about 42 months or 1260 days, as mentioned in Revelation 13:5.[3]

However, there are serious difficulties with identifying Nero with the beast who comes up out of the sea in Revelation 13. First, the book of Revelation was written in A.D. 95, after the reign of Nero was already over. Therefore, it can't be a prophecy about him.[4]

Second, preterists Gary DeMar and Kenneth Gentry take the 42 months of the beast's worldwide reign literally, and then turn around and take almost every other number in Revelation symbolically. Why take the 42 months literally and all the other numerical references symbolically? There is no justification within the text for this inconsistent approach to the interpretation of it.

Third, and most importantly, Nero never fulfilled many of the very clear statements present in Revelation 13. Here are just a few examples:

1. The beast will be worshiped by the *entire* world; "All who dwell on the earth will worship him, everyone whose name has not been written from the foundation of the world in the book of life of the Lamb who has been slain" (Revelation 13:8). All classes of humanity will be forced to take sides: "the small and the great, and the rich and the poor, and the free men and the slaves" (Revelation 13:16). Robert Thomas, a noted New Testament scholar, notes that this language "extends to all people of every civic rank...all classes ranked according to wealth...covers every cultural category...The three expressions are a formula for universality."[5]

2. He will force people to take his mark on their right hand or forehead to engage in any commercial transactions.

3. An image of the beast will be erected by the false prophet that all the world must worship.

4. The beast will be slain and come back to life.

5. The beast in Revelation 13:1-10 will have an

associate, the false prophet, who will call down
fire from heaven and give breath to the image.

Clearly, none of those prophecies were fulfilled during Nero's
reign. Neither Nero, nor any other Roman emperor, ever marked
the whole world with 666. But all of these prophecies will be fulfilled precisely with the coming Antichrist of the end times.

Fourth, in order for Nero's name to equal 666, you have to
use the precise title *Neron Ceasar*. No other form of his name
will work. Moreover, there is an abbreviated form of the name
Domitian (the Roman Caesar from A.D. 81–96) that also equals
666.[6]

Fifth, if the relationship of 666 to Nero is so obvious, as preterists claim, why did it take almost 1800 years after Nero's death for
anyone to make this connection between his name and 666?[7] All
the early church fathers who wrote after the time of Nero adopted
a futurist view of the beast out of the sea and the number 666.[8]
The first individuals to suggest a connection between Nero and
666 were four German scholars in the 1830s.[9]

Revelation 13:17-18 clearly says that the number 666 will be
the mark proposed for the right hand or forehead. No one in history, including Nero, ever proposed the use of such a number in
such a fashion in anything like Tribulation conditions, so past
guesses as to the Antichrist's identity can be nullified on this basis.
Robert Thomas provides wise guidance in this area:

> The better part of wisdom is to be content that the
> identification is not yet available, but will be when the
> future false Christ ascends to his throne. The person
> to whom 666 applies must have been future to John's
> time, because John clearly meant the number to be rec-
> ognizable to someone. If it was not discernible to his

generation and those immediately following him—and it was not—the generation to whom it will be discernible must have lain (and still lies) in the future. Past generations have provided many illustrations of this future personage, but all past candidates have proven inadequate as fulfillments.[10]

What Is the Mark of the Beast?

Having determined that this mark of the beast is future, the next thing we need to do is define the nature of this mark. The Bible teaches that during the future Tribulation period the false prophet, who will be the head of Antichrist's religious propaganda machine, will head up the campaign of the mark of the beast (Revelation 13:11-18). Revelation 13:15 makes it clear that the key issue underlying the mark of the beast is worship of the image of the beast. The mark of the beast is simply a vehicle to force people to declare their allegiance—to the Antichrist or Jesus Christ. All people will be polarized into two camps. It will be impossible to take a position of neutrality or indecision. Scripture is very clear that those who do not receive the mark will be killed (Revelation 20:4).

All classes of humanity will be forced to take sides: "the small and the great, and the rich and the poor, and the free men and the slaves" (Revelation 13:15). Scripture is very specific: the false prophet will require a "mark" of loyalty and devotion to the beast and it will be "on their right hand," not the left, "or on their forehead" (Revelation 13:16).

But what is this "mark"?

We find the word "mark" sprinkled throughout the Bible.

For example, it is used many times in Leviticus as a reference to a mark that renders the subject ceremonially unclean, usually in relation to leprosy. Clearly, in these cases in Leviticus, the "mark" is external and visible.

Interestingly, Ezekiel 9:4 uses "mark" similarly to the way it is used in Revelation: "The LORD said to him, 'Go through the midst of the city, even through the midst of Jerusalem, and put *a mark on the foreheads* of the men who sigh and groan over all the abominations which are being committed in its midst'" (emphasis added). Here the mark was one of preservation, similar to the way the blood on the doorposts spared the Israelites from the death angel who killed all the Egyptian firstborn in the tenth plague (Exodus 12:21-29). In Ezekiel, the mark is placed visibly on the forehead, which anticipates Revelation's use of the term.

Seven out of the eight instances of the word for "mark" or "sign" in the Greek New Testament appear in Revelation, and all refer to "the mark of the beast" (Revelation 13:16-17; 14:9,11; 16:2; 19:20; 20:4). The word "mark" in Greek (*charagma*) means "a mark or stamp engraved, etched, branded, cut, imprinted."[11] Robert Thomas explains how the word was used in ancient times:

> The mark must be some sort of branding similar to that given soldiers, slaves, and temple devotees in John's day. In Asia Minor, devotees of pagan religions delighted in the display of such a tattoo as an emblem of ownership by a certain god. In Egypt, Ptolemy Philopator I branded Jews, who submitted to registration, with an ivy leaf in recognition of their Dionysian worship (cf. 3 *Macc.* 2:29). This meaning resembles the long-time practice of carrying signs to advertise religious loyalties (cf. Isa. 44:5) and follows the habit of branding slaves with the name or special mark of their owners (cf. Gal.

6:17). *Charagma* ("mark") was a term for the images or names of emperors on Roman coins, so it fittingly could apply to the beast's emblem put on people.[12]

Henry Morris also provides an excellent description of the nature of the mark:

> The nature of the mark is not described, but the basic principle has been established for years in various nations. The social security card, the draft registration card, the practice of stenciling an inked design on the back of the hand, and various other devices are all forerunners of this universal branding. The word itself ("mark") is the Greek *charagma*. It is used only in Revelation, to refer to the mark of the beast (eight times), plus one time to refer to idols "graven by art and man's device" (Acts 17:29). The mark is something like an etching or a tattoo which, once inscribed, cannot be removed, providing a permanent (possibly eternal) identification as a follower of the beast and the dragon.[13]

The issue for each person alive during the Tribulation will be this: Will I swear allegiance to the man who claims to be God? Will I give up ownership of my life to him by taking his mark, or will I bow the knee to the true God and lose my right to buy and sell and even face beheading? (see Revelation 20:4). Taking the mark will ultimately be a spiritual decision; the economic benefits will be secondary.

What's the Significance of 666?

In the movie *The Omen*, Damien was born on June 6, at 6:00 (666) to symbolize his identification as the coming Antichrist.

Almost everyone, including the most biblically illiterate people, have heard something about 666 or the mark of the beast.

As you can imagine, there are several explanations for what 666 means. But I believe the best one is the use of a process called *gematria,* which refers to the numerical value of names. In gematria, a numerical value is attributed to each of the letters of the alphabet. If you want to find the numerical total of a word or name, you add together the numerical value of each of its letters. Clearly, in Revelation 13 some kind of numerical value for the beast's name is intended, because the person who has wisdom is to "calculate" or "count" the number.[14] To count the number of a name simply means to add up the numbers attached to all the letters in the name.[15]

Hebrew, Latin, Greek, and English all have numerical values for each letter in their alphabets. For example, each letter in the 22-letter Hebrew alphabet is assigned a numerical value as follows: 1, 2, 3, 4, 5, 6, 7, 8, 9, 10, 20, 30, 40, 50, 60, 70, 80, 90, 100, 200, 300, and 400.

Revelation 13:16-18 provides five key clues that aid in the interpretation of the mark of the beast—clues that I believe support the idea that gematria is involved. Read Revelation 13:16-18 again and notice the progression of the phrases:

1. "the name of the beast"
2. "the number of his name"
3. "the number of the beast"
4. "the number is that of a man"
5. "his number is six hundred and sixty-six"[16]

When these five clues are followed according to their logical progression, the number or mark of the beast is the number of a man who is the Antichrist or final world ruler. This number is the number of the Antichrist's own name.

As prophecy scholar Arnold Fruchtenbaum notes,

> In this passage whatever the personal name of the Antichrist will be, if his name is spelled out in Hebrew characters, the numerical value of his name will be 666. So this is the number that will be put on the worshipers of the Antichrist. Since a number of different calculations can equal 666, it is impossible to figure the name out in advance. But when he does appear, whatever his personal name will be, it will equal 666. Those who are wise (verse 18) at that time will be able to point him out.[17]

When the Antichrist begins to appear on the world scene at the beginning of the Tribulation, those who have understanding of God's Word will be able to identify him by the number of his name because numerical value of his name will be 666.

Many people have grossly misused gematria to apply it to the names of modern leaders to see if they could be the Antichrist. It has been applied to Henry Kissinger and Lyndon Johnson, and I have been told that both of their names equal 666. It has also been successfully tried out on JFK, Gorbachev, and Ronald Reagan. Supposedly the name Bill Gates III equals 666. The "name" MS DOS 6.21 equals 666, as do the "names" Windows 95 and System 7.0.

I recently received a call from a man who told me emphatically that Philip Borbon Carlos, son of Juan Carlos of Spain, is the Antichrist because each of his three names contains six letters. Phone books are full of names that, if converted to their numerical value, add up to 666. However, the wisdom of counting the name is not to be applied in our day, for that would be jumping the gun. Instead, it is to be applied by believers during the Tribulation. All the current speculation is foolish and should be avoided because the Antichrist will not be unveiled until the beginning of the Tribulation period (2 Thessalonians 2:2-3). At that time, people will be able to identify him because the numerical value of his name will be 666. And if you ever do figure out who the Antichrist is, I've got bad news for you: You've missed the rapture and been left behind.

Why 666?

One might ask, "Why did the Lord plan for Antichrist's name to equal 666?" Many prophecy teachers have pointed out that the three sixes refers to man's number, which is the number six, or one short of God's perfect number, seven. Remember, man was created on the sixth day. Prophecy scholar John Walvoord wrote,

> Though there may be more light cast on it at the time this prophecy is fulfilled, the passage itself declares that this number is "man's number." In the Book of Revelation, the number "7" is one of the most significant numbers, indicating perfection. Accordingly, there are seven seals, seven trumpets, seven bowls of the wrath of God, seven thunders, etc. This beast claims to be God, and if that were the case, he should be 777. This passage, in effect, says, No, you are only 666. You are short of deity even though you were originally created in the image and likeness of God. Most of the speculation on the meaning of this number is without profit or theological significance.[18]

M.R. DeHaan, the founder of Radio Bible Class, also held this position:

> Six is the number of man. Three is the number of divinity. Here is the interpretation. The beast will be a man who claims to be God. Three sixes imply that he is a false god and a deceiver, but he is nevertheless merely a man, regardless of his claims. Seven is the number of divine perfection, and 666 is one numeral short of seven. This man of sin will reach the highest peak of power and wisdom, but he will still be merely a man.[19]

It is interesting to me that the number of the name *Jesus,* in Greek, is 888, and each of His eight names in the New Testament (Lord, Jesus, Christ, Lord Jesus, Jesus Christ, Christ Jesus, Lord Christ, and Lord Jesus Christ) all have numerical values that are multiples of eight.[20] I don't believe this is a coincidence. Jesus is complete perfection, while man, apart from God, is complete, utter failure.

Adam, the first man, was created on the sixth day, while Jesus, the second man, was raised from the dead on Sunday, the "eighth day" of the week (the second first day of the week).[21]

What's the Purpose of the Mark?

The mark of the beast will serve two purposes during the Great Tribulation. First, as we have already noted, it will serve as a visible indicator of devotion to Antichrist. Antichrist's mark, the numerical value of his name, will be etched or imprinted on the right hand or forehead of those who bow the knee to his iron fist. The mark of the beast will be a satanic counterfeit of the seal of God on the foreheads of the saints, which is the seal of the Holy Spirit (see Revelation 7:3).[22] It will be a global pledge of allegiance.

Taking it will be a visible sign that the marked person has bought into the Antichrist's vision, platform, and purpose. For a person to take this mark will *not* be an inadvertent, casual, accidental act. Those who take it will make a deliberate choice; they will know exactly what it means when they choose to accept it.

Second, the mark will provide an economic benefit. It will be one's ticket or passport for business. It will be required for commercial transactions during the last half of the Tribulation (Revelation 13:17). It will be in place to make the global order possible and to make sure that anyone outside this system cannot buy or sell. This is another clear indication that the mark is literal and visible. After all, how can it serve as a ticket for commercial transactions if it's invisible?

Stop and think about it. This has been the dream of every tyrant down through history—to so totally control his subjects that he alone decides who can buy or sell. When the beast or Antichrist seizes power at the middle of the Tribulation, every person on earth will be faced with a monumental decision: Will they take the mark of the beast on their right hand or forehead, or will they refuse the mark and face death? Will they take the mark that is required for every private and public transaction, or will they stand firm and say no to Antichrist?

The Antichrist's economic policy will be very simple: Take my mark and worship me, or starve. People will be forced to make a spiritual decision to serve the Antichrist and worship the beast and his image. The far better choice will be to refuse Antichrist and starve or face beheading, because those who receive the mark will forfeit eternal life. All who take the mark of the beast will face the eternal judgment of God. Taking the mark will seal their everlasting doom. It will be an unpardonable, irreversible sin. Revelation 14:9-10 says clearly,

Another angel, a third one, followed them, saying with a loud voice, "If anyone worships the beast and his image, and receives a mark on his forehead or on his hand, he also will drink of the wine of the wrath of God, which is mixed in full strength in the cup of His anger; and he will be tormented with fire and brimstone in the presence of the holy angels and in the presence of the Lamb. And the smoke of their torment goes up forever and ever; they have no rest day and night, those who worship the beast and his image, and whoever receives the mark of his name."

This reveals again that taking the mark is not ultimately about economics. God does not condemn people for purely economic reasons. To take the mark is to make a conscious decision to worship the beast. Only those who worship him can receive the mark.

What Does the Mark Reveal About the Antichrist?

The Antichrist's mark reveals two facts about the Antichrist. First, the fact he can force the whole world to take his mark reveals he will truly possess worldwide power and authority. Only a truly totalitarian power could make everyone on the earth take this mark or be killed.

Second, the fact the mark is necessary for all transactions reveals the Antichrist will control the life of every person on Earth. John Walvoord wrote, "There is no doubt that with today's technology, a world ruler, who is in total control, would have the ability to keep a continually updated census of all living persons and know day-by-day precisely which people had pledged their allegiance to him and received the mark and which had not."[23]

Does Modern Technology Relate to the Mark of the Beast?

What will the mark of the beast look like? What form will it take? Will it be something as simple as a tattoo? Will it be some kind of ID card? Will it be a chip placed under the skin? In the aftermath of 9/11, some have called for some form of national ID card, biometric identification (thumbprint or eye scan), or digitizing or scanner technology to be instituted on all people nationwide.[24] Many have speculated whether one of these new technologies will be used for the mark of the beast. The mark has been related to Social Security cards, bar code scanners, retina scanners, the new Veri Chip implant technology, and just about every other kind of new identification technology that comes along. There have been all kinds of unwarranted speculations on the exact nature of the mark of the beast. As my friend Dr. Harold Willmington has said, "There's been a lot of sick, sick, sick about six, six, six."

When it comes to the exact nature of the mark of the beast, the answer is that we really don't know, and we shouldn't waste a lot of time thinking about it. Nothing that we see today is the mark of the beast. We don't know what method Antichrist will adopt to make his mark. The text of Revelation 13:16 clearly indicates that the mark will be placed "on" or "upon" the hand or forehead, not "in" it—that is, on the outside, where it can be seen. The Greek preposition *epi*, in this context, means "upon."

What we can safely and responsibly say is that the technology is certainly available today to tattoo, brand, or partially embed a visible identifying number or mark on the skin of every person alive to regulate world commerce and control people's lives. While none of the things we see today are the mark of the beast, the rise of these amazing new means of locating, identifying, and controlling people's lives strikingly foreshadows the scenario depicted in Revelation 13. It's just another indicator that points toward the picture Scripture paints of the end times.

How Will the Antichrist Do It?

I don't know if you've ever thought about this before, but I've often wondered how the Antichrist will convince people to accept his mark. After all, most people, even those with little or no biblical background, have heard about 666 and know that it's an evil sign. There are hundreds of thousands of websites that discuss the mysterious mark. Anyone who has seen popular movies such as *The Omen* or even has a passing interest in rock music has heard of the number 666 and its association with the Antichrist. The day after Barak Obama, a senator from Illinois, was elected president, the winning number in the Evening Pick 3 Illinois lottery was 6-6-6, leading some to irresponsibly view this as a harbinger that he's the Antichrist. After all, the same number combination had already shown up three other times earlier that year. The point is this: People everywhere know something about 666.

Given this widespread awareness, how will the Antichrist convince billions of people to receive the mark on their bodies? Surely he would be shrewd enough to use 665 or 667 or any number besides the notorious 666.

One possible scenario is that the Antichrist will be so bold, blasphemous, and arrogant that he will be able to use his charisma and mesmerizing oratory to convince people to take this taboo mark. Though people will know it's an affront to God, they will take the mark anyway and openly rebel against God.

Another possibility is that the Antichrist will use the rapture of the church, the disappearance of millions of people, to play on people's fears. He may claim to be the only one on Earth with the true explanation for what happened to all the people. He may even claim to be the source of the disappearances and threaten those who rebel against him that they too will disappear. He may issue some kind of guarantee that no more people will disappear as long as they comply with him and are registered with his mark. Only then can they avoid being "vaporized." In this way he will get the whole world to unite under his political, economic, and religious system.

Another possible explanation is found in 2 Thessalonians 2:9-11:

> The one whose coming is in accord with the activity of Satan, with all power and signs and false wonders, and with all the deception of the wickedness for those who perish, because they did not receive the love of the truth so as to be saved. For this reason God will send upon them a deluding influence so that they might believe what is false, in order that they all may be judged who did not believe the truth, but took pleasure in wickedness.

During the coming Tribulation, the Antichrist will be empowered by Satan to perform incredible signs and wonders that will amaze and dumbfound even the most sophisticated people. His deception will create awe and wonder that will draw billions of people to turn to him as a savior. Those who turn from the truth of God to Antichrist and refuse God's gracious offer of salvation will be turned over to their own self-willed choice. God will confirm their choice and send a deluding influence on them so that they will receive, literally, "the lie." What is the lie? The belief that the Antichrist is God. So even those people who are familiar with the number 666 and its evil connotations will gladly accept it and all it represents. The strong delusion will overcome any hesitation they might have about receiving the mark of the beast.

What Does All This Mean?

We've just answered eight questions that have helped us to better understand the mark of the beast. Here is a summary of the meaning of the mark of the beast and the application for our lives today:

1. The mark is future, not past.

2. The mark is a literal, visible brand, mark, or tattoo that will be placed "on" the right hand or forehead of people during the Great Tribulation.

3. The mark will be given as a sign of devotion to Antichrist and as a passport to engage in commerce.

4. The mark will be the number 666, which will be the numerical value of the Antichrist's name. This information will enable the saints who are alive at the time of the Tribulation to "calculate the number of the beast" and identify him.

5. Those who take the mark will be eternally doomed.

6. Until the rapture has taken place, no one should attempt to identify the Antichrist or his mark—the number 666.

7. While the latest technological methods of identifying and locating people strikingly foreshadow Antichrist's ability to control the world, it is not possible

to determine which technology will be employed to fulfill this prophecy. But the technology that's now available certainly makes the implementation of such a system not only possible, but probable.

8. In spite of its association with evil, the number 666 will be received by those who willfully reject God.

Hitting the Mark

As amazing as the idea of the mark of the beast is, there's something much more stunning to be noticed here that we dare not miss. The Bible predicted the usage of this mark over 1900 years ago. The fact that the words of Revelation 13 were penned in the age of wood, stones, swords, spears, and Roman togas makes this prophecy one of the most powerful proofs that God's Word can be trusted. Who could have predicted a one-world economic system that controls all commerce but God? As God says, "I am God, and there is no other; I am God, and there is no one like Me, declaring the end from the beginning, and from ancient times things which have not been done" (Isaiah 46:9-10). The astounding prophecy about the mark of the beast—which is able to be fulfilled with today's technology—is just one more compelling piece of evidence that the God of the Bible is the true and living God and that the Bible is His inspired, inerrant Word.

12

MEGATREND 20/20: SEEING THE FUTURE CLEARLY

How Close Is Cashless?

> "Current events will shape not only our
> immediate financial prospects, but the
> global economy for decades to come."
>
> LIAM HALLIGAN

When we look at our world today, events are unfolding exactly as one would expect if the prophecies of the Bible are true. On every front, it looks like the Lord is positioning the world for the end times. Here are just a few of the major signs of the times that are developing before our eyes:

- Israel is regathered back in the Promised Land after almost 2000 years, surrounded by a sea of enemies who want to wipe the nation off the map.

- After the passage of 1600 years, the old Roman Empire appears to be coming back together in the form of the European Union (EU).

- The entire world is focused on the Middle East due to terrorism and oil.

- The world, which is becoming more dangerous and unstable, is desperately yearning for peace, especially in the Middle East. The prophet Daniel predicted that a seven-year peace treaty with Israel will usher in the end times (Daniel 9:27).

- Russia ("Rosh") is the great regional power mentioned in Ezekiel 38.

- Iran ("Persia"), identified in Ezekiel 38:5 as one of the leaders of an end-time invasion of Israel, has risen to become one of the most powerful nations in the Middle East and harbors a venomous hatred for Israel.

- The other nations mentioned in Ezekiel 38:1-6 are identifiable nations with the will and means to attack Israel.

What's more, the global financial meltdown—or "Great Recession"—that the world has experienced has been seized by globalists as an opportunity to centralize economic power within the United States and to more deeply intertwine the economies of the world. Globalism is the new world order. The world is on the fast track to a global economy. There is no turning back. It's no longer a matter of *if*, but *when*. The trends we are witnessing in that direction are shocking in their suddenness and scope. It appears that this key sign of the end times is yet another significant indicator that the world is well down the road to Armageddon.

Key Points to Remember

Up to this point, we have covered quite a lot of ground, so I thought it might be helpful to pause for a moment to briefly summarize and review what we've covered. To make sure we have a firm grasp of how current headlines, the Bible, and end-time events fit together, here is a condensed summary that I hope will pull together the major threads of thought we've covered.

1. According to Revelation 13 and 18, there will be a one-world economic system in the end times.

2. This end-time economic system will probably involve a one-world currency.

3. Some form of a cashless system will be used, backed up by biometrics, in order to assure accurate identification and centralized, complete control.

4. After the rapture of all true believers to heaven, a group of ten leaders will emerge from a reunited Roman Empire to stop the world chaos and bring stability. Then one man who has extraordinary abilities will be elected the chairman of this group. The Bible calls him the Antichrist.

5. A devastating global financial crisis, predicted in Revelation 6:5-6, will cause the entire global system to collapse, will trigger massive unemployment and famine, and will pave the way for the Antichrist to take control.

6. In the wake of this crisis, the Antichrist will seize control of the world economy, which will likely be experiencing hyperinflation.

7. The Antichrist's economic czar and "worship leader," known as the false prophet, will require the mark of the beast as an outward, visible sign of allegiance to the Antichrist and a passport for participation in global commerce.

8. Current global financial trends strikingly fore-shadow the coming of a cashless society.

Are You Ready?

The bottom line is this: The current economic crisis appears to be a significant prelude to the one-world economy the Bible predicted almost 2000 years ago. For one man to control the world economy there must be a global, unified system that is cashless and has the ability to identify every person and control all supply and demand. That is now possible. This stunning development, when viewed in light of the convergence of so many other signs of the times, leads me to believe that the coming of the Lord could be very near. The end-time signposts are lined up.

There will certainly be many twists and turns before the dust finally settles and the final form of the one-world financial system takes shape. No one knows what precise processes will bring it to life or when it will be established. But, make no mistake, it will come. The astonishing prophecies of Revelation 13:16-18 and Revelation 18 will be just as literally fulfilled as the hundreds of biblical prophecies that have already been literally fulfilled.

The question each of us faces is this: Am I ready for the future? God gave us the astounding prophecies about the last days not to scare us but to prepare us. Are you prepared?

Are you ready for the coming of the Lord?

13

Cashless and You

Dollars and Sense

"Would it not be high tragedy if our affluent society collapsed into unexpected bankruptcy because, by exploring one world only, it lost the real world of tomorrow and the enduring world of eternity."

CARL F.H. HENRY

Earlier in this book, I noted that many people view times of crisis as seasons of opportunity. As we have seen, political and financial opportunists have already seized the current world financial crisis to push their global agenda. We can expose their actions and examine the biblical significance of what we see, and it's important to do so. But as we scan the horizon of the future, we dare not let this season pass without also stopping to think about what the Lord would teach us for our own lives today. I believe that the current economic crisis, while devastating and trying for us all, also carries with it the rare opportunity for each of us to do some much-needed soul searching and re-evaluation. There are several important lessons that we dare not miss; let me suggest six very practical applications for you to consider.

The Final Invitation

First, if you have never personally accepted Jesus Christ as your Savior from sin, then you need to do it right now. Accept the pardon that Jesus purchased for you when He died on the cross in your place. He offers it to you free of charge. I think it's beautiful that the last verses in the final book of the Bible ends with an open invitation, a call to receive God's free gift of eternal life. "The Spirit and the bride say, 'Come.' And let the one who hears say, 'Come.' And let the one who is thirsty come; let the one who wishes take the water of life without cost" (Revelation 22:17). God offers the water of life free of charge to any thirsty soul who will simply take it. It's free, but you have to take it.

Years ago I heard a story about Dr. Walter Wilson of Kansas City. Dr. Wilson, who was a medical doctor and evangelist, was preaching at a church on the final night of a week-long series of meetings. He was trying his best to make the message of the gospel crystal clear so everyone there could understand God's plan of salvation. At the end of the meeting, Dr. Wilson said, "Let's pretend you are very sick, and the only thing that will cure your illness is this medicine here that I prescribe for you. Now, let me ask you a question. Will the medicine do you any good?"

There was a prolonged, uncomfortable silence in the church auditorium. Finally, a young boy in the back couldn't stand it any longer and hollered out, "Not unless you take it!"

Dr. Wilson's face lit up. He said, "That's exactly right. It won't do you a bit of good unless you take it."

I realize that story is very simple, but my point in sharing it is to say that if you have never accepted Christ, you need to take the free gift of eternal life right now. Every person who has not accepted Christ as their Savior has a very serious problem—a sin problem. It's fatal, deadly, and eternal in its consequences. But God has just the remedy for the problem. Jesus paid it all. He died for your sins on the cross and rose again from the dead as proof that God accepted in full the payment that He made. Now all you have to do is take it. John 1:12 says, "To all who believed him and accepted him, he gave the right to become the children of God" (NLT).

God promises in His Word that "whoever will call on the name of the Lord will be saved" (Romans 10:13). Why not call on Him in faith right now, accepting Christ and His gifts of forgiveness of sin and eternal life? There are no magic words to say, but you might want to call upon the Lord with the simple words of this prayer:

> Lord, I admit that I am a sinner. I have gone my own way in life and have broken Your laws and commands. I recognize that I cannot save myself by my own good works. I must have a Savior. And I believe that Jesus Christ is the Savior who died for me on the cross and rose again. I now receive Him by faith, trusting in Him alone for salvation from sin. Thank You for the free gift of salvation through Christ. Amen.

If you have prayed this prayer, let someone know. Find a loving, Bible-teaching church to attend. And find a way to serve the Lord and live your life for Him who gave His life for you.

The Current Christless Society

Second, while it is essential to understand as much as we can about Bible prophecy, we must never get so focused on the future and end-time events that we lose sight of today's Christless society.[1] Every person who is a Christian needs to pray for open doors of opportunity to share the gospel of Jesus Christ with others and the boldness to seize those opportunities. In difficult times, many people who otherwise might be closed to the truth about Jesus might suddenly display a surprising openness to spiritual issues. May the Holy Spirit energize us and awaken us to be sensitive to the open doors all around us.

Lessons from Laodicea

A third important lesson in times like these is the need to recognize that an inordinate focus on money and materialism can greatly hinder our usefulness to the Lord and disrupt our fellowship with Him. Christ's message to the first-century church of Laodicea serves as a stirring wake-up call to contemporary Western Christianity, whose followers are often smug, self-sufficient, and secure in their material wealth:

> I know your deeds, that you are neither cold nor hot; I wish that you were cold or hot. So because you are lukewarm and neither hot nor cold, I will spit [vomit] you out of My mouth. Because you say, "I am rich, and have become wealthy, and have need of nothing," and you do not know that you are wretched and miserable and poor and blind and naked, I advise you to buy from Me gold refined by fire so that you may become rich, and white garments so that you may clothe yourself, and

that the shame of your nakedness may not be revealed;
and eye salve to anoint your eyes so that you may see.
Those whom I love, I reprove and discipline; therefore
be zealous and repent. Behold, I stand at the door and
knock; if anyone hears My voice and opens the door,
I will come in to him and will dine with him, and he
with Me (Revelation 3:15-20).

A focus on material riches had caused the members of the Laodicean church to be lukewarm. Hot and cold fluids are both good for something. We like hot coffee or cold soda. A hot bath is relaxing; a cold dip in the pool is refreshing. But lukewarm liquids are useless. They aren't good for anything. Jesus is saying that inordinate focus and reliance on riches deludes us into a false sense of self-sufficiency and renders us lukewarm—useless for Him to use.

A true believer in Christ never loses his or her salvation, but can certainly become useless to the Lord. The answer to this problem is found in the searching words of Revelation 3:19-20: "Those whom I love, I reprove and discipline; therefore be zealous and repent. Behold, I stand at the door and knock; if anyone hears My voice and opens the door, I will come in to him and will dine with him, and he with Me." When a person senses that he has fallen into Laodicean laxity, he needs to repent or do a 180-degree turn and open the door of his heart to the seeking Savior and re-establish intimate fellowship with Him. He's always ready to welcome us back, love us, and begin to use us again.

Open Heart, Open Hands

Fourth, a time of financial reversal should cause us to think long and hard about what we do with our money. Do we spend it all on ourselves and our own pursuits, or do we gladly share it generously with others? Do we prayerfully consider how the Lord would have us spend the resources He has committed to our care?

May the Lord help us to be generous, gracious, sacrificial givers who joyfully give back to the One who has given us every good and perfect gift, especially the indescribable gift of His Son (2 Corinthians 9:15).

Slave or Master?

Fifth, money is a great slave but a terrible master. Many people have learned this lesson the hard way. Have we thoughtlessly and selfishly laid up more and more treasure for ourselves on Earth for the purpose of acquiring more security and significance? Have we fallen into the trap of thinking that what we have belongs to us? Or do we understand that we are simply temporary managers of God's resources for our brief time on earth? Take some time to read and meditate on Luke 12:13-21, Matthew 6:19-34, and 1 Timothy 6:7-10. Remember that ultimately, you will master your money, or your money will master you.

What Money Cannot Buy

Sixth, we need to beware of the way wrong priorities in the area of finances can warp and cloud our thinking. Greed and love of money and the things it can buy can make us self-centered and self-focused. There's a well-known story that emphasizes the importance making sense out of our dollars. A rich old man with a miserable outlook one day visited a rabbi. Knowing who the man was and his reputation for a foul disposition, the rabbi led him to a window.

"Look out there," said the rabbi, and the rich man glanced into the street.

"What do you see?" asked the rabbi.

"I see men, women and children," said the rich man.

The rabbi then took him by the hand and led him to a mirror.

"Now what do you see?" asked the rabbi.

"Now I see myself," the rich man replied.

Then the rabbi said, "Behold, in the window there is glass, and in the mirror there is glass. But the glass of the mirror is covered with a little silver, and no sooner is the silver added than you cease to see others, but only yourself."

This same principle is true when it comes to seeing God. Money and material wealth can easily lead us to the place where we no longer see the Lord, but only ourselves. As Thomas Ice and Timothy Demy poignantly observe,

> In our society, as well as in a potential cashless society, money will buy a bed, but not rest; food, but not satisfaction; luxury, but not contentment; stocks, but not security; a house, but not a home; sedatives, but not a Savior...What money cannot buy, God offers without charge. Making dollars and making sense are sometimes two very different things. Jesus offered us an interesting challenge in perspective and priority when He asked, "For what will it profit a man to gain the whole world and forfeit his soul?" (Mark 8:36).[2]

In these days of economic crisis, may the Lord help us to discern the difference between dollars and sense. And may we live like people who are waiting for their Master to return so that we are ready when He comes.

It may be very soon!

APPENDIXES

APPENDIX A:

Some Questions You Might Be Asking

In most of my books I like to anticipate some of the questions that readers might have or provide further background information about the subjects addressed. This book discusses the Antichrist and his coming world economic system in some detail, and here is some additional material you might find helpful, which is presented in a question-answer format.

1. What did the early church believe about the Antichrist?

Some claim that the idea of a personal, end-time Antichrist is a modern myth.[1] But is it? Of course, what ultimately matters is what the Bible says about the Antichrist, not people. But it's always helpful to see what others in the history of the church have said about any given issue. After all, there is wisdom in standing on the shoulders of those who have gone before us.

The evidence reveals that the notion of an end-time Antichrist goes all the way back to the earliest days of the church. Here is a brief outline of what the early church believed about the Antichrist:

The *Didache,* or Teaching of the Twelve Apostles, was written sometime between A.D. 70–100. This early church document recognized the coming of a personal Antichrist who would bring a time of unparalleled trouble on the earth.

> For as lawlessness increases, they will hate and persecute and betray one another. And then the deceiver of the world will appear as a son of God and "will perform signs and wonders," and the earth will be delivered into his hands, and he will commit abominations the likes of which have never happened before.[2]

Irenaeus was the premier Christian thinker of the second century A.D. He included a treatment on the Antichrist in his great work *Against Heresies.* In that work he detailed his view of the coming evil one:

- Antichrist is a single individual whose coming was still future in the second century A.D.
- He will totally embody evil, just as Christ does good.[3]
- Antichrist will be a Jew from the tribe of Dan.[4]
- Antichrist will reign over the world for a period of three-and-a-half years.[5]

Hippolytus was presbyter of Rome from about A.D. 200–235.

He wrote the first surviving, complete Christian biblical commentary, titled *Commentary on Daniel.* It was written about A.D. 204. He also penned an entire treatise concerning Antichrist, called *On the Antichrist.* Hippolytus listed six ways in which Antichrist will be a perverted imitation of Christ: 1) he will be of Jewish origin; 2) he will send out apostles; 3) he will bring together people spread abroad; 4) he will seal his followers; 5) he will appear in the form of a man; and 6) he will build a temple in Jerusalem.[6] Hippolytus also taught that Antichrist would rise from a ten-kingdom form of the Roman Empire, that he would rebuild the Roman Empire, that his career would last for three-and-a-half years, and that he would persecute Christians who refuse to worship him.[7]

Tertullian was the first major voice in Latin Christianity; he lived from about A.D. 160–220. Tertullian made it clear he believed both in present "antichrists," who were heretics who divided the church, and in a coming final Antichrist, who will persecute God's people.[8]

Cyril, bishop of Jerusalem, lived from about A.D. 315–386. Based on Daniel 7:13-27, 2 Thessalonians 2:4, and other passages about the Antichrist, Cyril expected a single Antichrist who will be a powerful, skilled worker of magic and sorcery. He will be the eleventh king of the fragmented Roman Empire and will rebuild the destroyed Jewish temple and enthrone himself there as God.[9]

Jerome (331–420), the great Latin father of the church, also believed in a personal Antichrist. Jerome too believed Antichrist would be a Jew, but Jerome also held that he would be born of a virgin and indwelt by Satan himself. He taught that the Roman Empire would be partitioned by ten kings who would be overcome by Antichrist, the eleventh king. He also believed the Antichrist would die on the Mount of Olives, the same place where Christ ascended to heaven.[10]

Bernard McGinn, a noted expert on the Antichrist, quotes David Dunbar, a renowned patristic scholar, who says that a "kind of mainline eschatology" had developed that was

> quite widespread during the closing decades of the second century. This mainline view in the church was that Antichrist would be a future Jewish individual from the tribe of Dan; he will come after the fragmentation of the Roman empire; he will be a persecuting tyrant; he will rebuild the temple in Jerusalem; he will exalt himself as god; he will rule for three and a half years; his fall will usher in Christ's return to earth.[11]

McGinn concludes: "These Christian fathers still offer food for thought to those at the end of the twentieth century who have lost belief in any literal Final Opponent."[12]

While the Bible, not church history, is our final authority concerning the doctrine of the Antichrist, we discover that church history solidly validates the idea of a personal, future Antichrist who will rule the world.

2. Will believers know who the Antichrist is?

The identity of Antichrist has intrigued people for 2000 years. Many have found the temptation to identify the Antichrist irresistible. There have been numerous candidates: the papacy, Emperor Frederick II, Pope Innocent IV, Muhammad, the Turks, Napoleon, Hitler, Mussolini, Stalin, Mikhail Gorbachev (whom some said had the mark of the beast on his forehead), Bill Clinton, or whomever the person claiming to identify the Antichrist happens to dislike.

As alluring as it may be at times to point someone out as the man of sin, we must avoid this temptation. Those who have given in to this temptation often draw a great deal of attention for awhile, but when they are proven wrong, they become examples of the danger of trying to identify the Antichrist before the proper time.

There is a key Scripture passage in the New Testament, 2 Thessalonians 2:1-8, that I believe teaches us that the rapture must come before the revelation of Antichrist. In other words, Christians cannot know who the Antichrist is before they are raptured to heaven.

Let's look briefly at 2 Thessalonians 2:1-8 and see what it teaches us about the relationship between the rapture and the appearance of Antichrist.

The Day of the Lord

The apostle Paul wrote 2 Thessalonians to the Thessalonian believers in northern Greece to clear up some confusion they had about the coming day of the Lord (which I believe begins with the seven-year Tribulation period). Evidently, someone had taught them that they were already in the Tribulation. Paul corrects this error by pointing out that the day of the Lord can't come until two things happen: a great apostasy or rebellion, and the revelation of the Antichrist or the man of lawlessness.

Second Thessalonians 2:1-3 says,

> Now we request you, brethren, with regard to the coming of our Lord Jesus Christ and our gathering together to Him, that you not be quickly shaken from your composure or be disturbed either by a spirit or a message or a letter as if from us, to the effect that the day of the Lord has come. Let no one in any way deceive you, for it will not come unless the apostasy comes first, and the man of lawlessness is revealed, the son of destruction.

Since, as I believe, the Antichrist will be revealed at the beginning of "the day of the Lord" (the Tribulation period), and the church will be raptured before this time, it doesn't appear that Christians will know the identity of the Antichrist before they are taken to heaven.

Sometime after the rapture, the Antichrist will come on the scene to sign his seven-year peace covenant with Israel, and then the Tribulation will begin. No doubt the chaos and confusion created by the disappearance of millions of people worldwide at the rapture will make the environment ripe for the Antichrist to rise quickly to the top. The world will be desperate for answers and for someone who can bring order. The Antichrist will catapult onto the scene with answers, but the honeymoon won't last long because the world will be plunged into the Tribulation.

The Removal of the Restrainer

In 2 Thessalonians 2, the apostle Paul said the Antichrist cannot be revealed until "he who now restrains" is taken out of the way. This restrainer is referred to both as a person and a power:

> Let no one in any way deceive you, for it will not come
> unless the apostasy comes first, and the man of lawless-
> ness is revealed, the son of destruction, who opposes
> and exalts himself above every so-called god or object of
> worship, so that he takes his seat in the temple of God,
> displaying himself as being God. Do you not remember
> that while I was still with you, I was telling you these
> things? And you know what restrains him now, so that
> in his time he will be revealed. For the mystery of law-
> lessness is already at work; only he who now restrains will
> do so until he is taken out of the way. Then that lawless
> one will be revealed whom the Lord will slay with the

breath of His mouth and bring to an end by the appearance of His coming (2 Thessalonians 2:3-8).

God is telling us that one thing in particular is hindering the full outbreak of evil and the opening of the door for Antichrist's entrance onto the world stage. And this hindrance is called "he who restrains now," or the restrainer. While there are many explanations for the identity of the restrainer, I believe the best view is that the restrainer is the Holy Spirit working in and through the church, the body of Christ on Earth.[13]

There are four reasons for identifying "he who now restrains" or the restrainer as the Holy Spirit and His restraining influence upon the evil in this world:

1. This restraint requires omnipotent power. The only One with the power to restrain and hold back the appearance of Antichrist is God.

2. This is the only view that adequately explains the change in gender in 2 Thessalonians 2:6-7. The restrainer is both a power—"what restrains him now," and a person—"he who now restrains." In the original Greek text, the word *pneuma* (Spirit) is neuter. But the Holy Spirit is also consistently referred to by the masculine pronoun "He," especially in John 14–16.

3. The Holy Spirit is spoken of in Scripture as restraining sin and evil in the world (Genesis 6:3) and in the heart of the believer (Galatians 5:16-17).

4. The church and its mission of proclaiming and portraying the gospel is the primary instrument the Holy Spirit uses in this age to restrain evil. Christians are the salt of the earth and the light of the

world (Matthew 5:13-16). They are the temple of
the Holy Spirit both individually and corporately.

The restrainer, then, is the Holy Spirit and the church. The
Holy Spirit indwells and works through His people in this present age to hold back the influence of evil. I love the description of
the identity of the restrainer by the famous Bible teacher Donald
Grey Barnhouse:

> Well, what is keeping the Antichrist from putting in
> his appearance on the world stage? *You* are! You and
> every other member of the body of Christ on earth. The
> presence of the church of Jesus Christ is the restrain-
> ing force that refuses to allow the man of lawlessness
> to be revealed. True, it is the Holy Spirit who is the
> real restrainer. But as both 1 Corinthians 3:16 and 6:19
> teach, the Holy Spirit indwells the believer. The believer's
> body is the temple of the Spirit of God. Put all believers
> together then, with the Holy Spirit indwelling each of
> us, and you have a formidable restraining force.
>
> For when the church is removed at the rapture, the
> Holy Spirit goes with the church insofar as His restrain-
> ing power is concerned. His work in this age of grace
> will be ended. Henceforth, during the Great Tribulation,
> the Holy Spirit will still be here on earth, of course—
> for how can you get rid of God?—but He will not be
> indwelling believers as He does now. Rather, He will
> revert to His Old Testament ministry of "coming upon"
> special people.[14]

When the rapture occurs, the Spirit-indwelt church and its
restraining influence will be removed. Satan will then be able
to put his plan into full swing by bringing his man onto center

stage to take control of the world. The rapture will remove the one hindrance to the full outbreak of evil in the world and throw the door wide open for Antichrist to come to power.

Looking for Christ

We must remember this important fact: The Antichrist will not be revealed until after the church is taken to heaven. Therefore, no one can know the identity of the Antichrist until we are raptured to heaven. That's why believers are never told to look for Antichrist, but for Christ.

We are looking for the One whose name is above every name, before whom every knee will bow and every tongue will confess that He is Lord, to the glory of God the Father (Philippians 2:9-11).

3. Will the Antichrist die and come back to life?

Several places in this book I briefly mentioned the fact that the Antichrist will die and come back to life. He will parody Christ so completely that he will actually die and come back to life. Here is what we are told in Revelation 13:3-4:

> I saw one of his heads as if it had been slain, and his fatal wound was healed. And the whole earth was amazed and followed after the beast; they worshiped the dragon because he gave his authority to the beast; and they worshiped the beast, saying, "Who is like the beast, and who is able to wage war with him?"

Some maintain that the Antichrist will not actually die and come back to life. Apologist Hank Hanegraaff deems such a notion preposterous. He says,

If Antichrist could rise from the dead and control the earth and sky…Christianity would lose the basis for believing that Christ's resurrection vindicated His claim to deity. In a Christian worldview, Satan can parody the work of Christ through "all kinds of counterfeit miracles, signs and wonders" (2 Thessalonians 2:9), but he cannot perform the truly miraculous as Christ did. If Satan possesses the creative power of God, he could have masqueraded as the resurrected Christ. Moreover, the notion that Satan can perform acts that are indistinguishable from genuine miracles suggests a dualistic worldview in which God and Satan are equal powers competing for dominance.[15]

Hanegraaff further states: "What is at stake here is nothing less than the deity and resurrection of Christ. In a Christian worldview, only God has the power to raise the dead."[16]

Parody or Reality?

Is the resurrection of the beast during the Tribulation for real, or is it just a cheap trick? I believe that the signs, wonders, and miracles done through satanic agency are indeed miraculous. Jesus (Matthew 24:4-5,11,24), Paul (2 Thessalonians 2:9), and John (Revelation 13:13-15; 16:13-14; 19:20) all describe miraculous works accomplished through Satan's oversight, and they use the very same language used of miracles performed by Jesus Himself. It appears that during the Tribulation, when the restrainer will be removed, satanic power will be unleashed upon the Earth as never before. God the Holy Spirit is now restraining "the man of lawlessness" (2 Thessalonians 2:3) from certain activity during the current era (2 Thessalonians 2:6-7). Once the Holy Spirit steps aside, satanic activity will dramatically increase. The Antichrist's coming "is in accord with the activity of Satan, with all power and signs and false wonders" (2 Thessalonians 2:9). Paul specifically says of this activity that it is something God will send (2 Thessalonians 2:11). The purpose is "so that they will believe what is false, in order that they all may be judged who did not believe the truth, but took pleasure in wickedness" (2 Thessalonians 2:11-12).

Let's consider a few reasons it appears that the beast will rise from the dead and do genuine miracles during the Tribulation.

Signs, Wonders, and Miracles

The primary language used in Scripture to describe the miracles of Christ and the apostles are the terms "signs," "wonders," and "miracles." The Greek word for "sign" is *semeion* and means "sign" or "distinguishing mark" by which something is known. It is used of miracles by Christ and the apostles in many passages (Matthew 12:38; 16:1,4; Mark 8:11-12; 16:17,20; Luke 11:16,29; 23:8; John 2:11,18,23; 3:2; 4:48,54; 6:2,14,26,30; 7:31; 9:16; Acts 2:22,43; 4:16,30; 5:12; 6:8; 7:36; 14:3; 15:12; Romans 15:19; 1 Corinthians 1:22; 2 Corinthians 12:12; Hebrews 2:4).[17] This is the most common word used to describe the miraculous works of Christ and His apostles.

In the New Testament, miracles are also referred to by the Greek word *teras,* which is translated into English as "a wonder, marvel."[18] The noun "wonder" occurs 16 times in the New Testament and is always coupled with the word "sign" (Matthew 24:24; Mark 13:22; John 4:48; Acts 2:19,22,43; 4:30; 5:12; 6:8; 7:36; 14:3; 15:12; Romans 15:19; 2 Corinthians 12:12; 2 Thessalonians 2:9; Hebrews 2:4). All but 2 Thessalonians 2:9 describes the miracles done by Christ and the apostles and notes "something so strange as to cause it to be 'watched' or 'observed.'"[19]

The remaining Greek words used of miracles are *dunamis* and *energeia,* which are usually translated as "miracle" and "working." "Both point more to the supernatural source rather than to what is produced,"[20] concludes Gregory M. Harris. Other than in 2 Thessalonians 2:9, these words always refer to "the workings of God."[21] Philip Edgcumbe Hughes ties it all together with the following statement:

> It is best to take signs, wonders, and miracles as belonging together rather than as indicating three different forms of manifestation...Thus a sign, which is the word consistently used in the Fourth Gospel for the miraculous works of Christ, indicates that the event is not an empty ostentation of power, but is significant in that, sign-wise, it points beyond itself to the reality of the mighty hand of God in operation. A wonder is an event which, because of its superhuman character, excites awe and amazement on the part of the beholder. A miracle (or literally power) emphasizes the dynamic character of the event, with particular regard to its outcome or effect.[22]

Amazingly, the words just noted to express the miraculous works of Christ and the apostles are also the terms used to describe "the miracles performed in the Tribulation by those in allegiance with Satan."[23] "Signs" is used of satanic miracles during the Tribulation (Revelation 13:13-14; 16:14), "and the same combination of words is used: great signs and wonders (Matthew 24:24: Mark 13:22), all power and signs and wonder (2 Thessalonians 2:9)."[24] Of special note is 2 Thessalonians 2:9, which says of the man of lawlessness that he is "the one whose coming is in accord with the activity of Satan, with all power and signs and false wonders."

It sounds like the Bible is telling us that these are miracles, similar to the ones done by our Lord. "The word *pseudos* ('false') has to do with the results of the miracles, not with their lack of genuineness or supernatural origin."[25] The language used by the inspired New Testament writers will not allow for a meaning that these satanic works are just sleight-of-hand magic tricks, as we shortly will see.

> Then that lawless one will be revealed whom the Lord will slay with the breath of His mouth and bring to an end by the appearance of His coming; that is, the one whose coming is in accord with the activity of Satan, with all power and signs and false wonders, and with all the deception of wickedness for those who perish, because they did not receive the love of the truth so as to be saved. For this reason God will send upon them a deluding influence so that they might believe what is false, in order that they all may be judged who did not believe the truth, but took pleasure in wickedness (2 Thessalonians 2:8-12).

Bible passages use the exact same vocabulary to refer to satanic miracles performed through the Antichrist and the false prophet as was used to refer to the miracles of Jesus and His disciples. This fact supports the notion that the Tribulation is a unique time in history during which God will permit Satan to do miracles so he can deceive those who are rejecting Christ's salvation.

Identical Language

Revelation 13 tells us much about the beast (also known as the Antichrist) and the false prophet. This chapter tells us the beast will have a "fatal wound" that is "healed" (verse 3). The chapter also says that the false prophet will make "the earth and those who dwell in it to worship the first beast, whose fatal wound was healed" (verse 12). He will perform "great signs, so that he even makes fire come down out of heaven to the earth in the presence of men" (verse 13). He will deceive "those who dwell on the earth because of the signs which it was given him to perform in the presence of the beast, telling those who dwell on the earth to make an image to the beast who had the wound of the sword and has come to life" (verse 14). He will also "give breath to the image of the beast, so that the image of the beast would even speak" (verse 15).

Charles Ryrie notes, "The Greek phrase used in verses 3 and 12…describes the fatal wound to the Beast. Revelation 5:6 describes the Lamb as if slain (*hos esphagmenen*), the same words used of the wound received by the beast (*hos esphagmenen*) in Revelation 13:3)." Because of this close similarity, Ryrie concludes, "If Christ died actually, then it appears that this ruler will also actually die. But his wound would be healed, which can only mean restoration to life."[26]

Furthermore, "the word referring to the beast's return to life is similar to the word used of Christ's return to life. Jesus is the One 'who was dead and has come to life [*ezesen*]' (2:8). And the beast will be the one 'who had the wound of the sword and has come to life [*ezesen*]' (13:14)."[27]

In support of this understanding is the fact that Revelation 17:8,11 refers to the beast that "was and is not." Harris notes, "This may well refer to the wounding of the Antichrist in 13:3, 12, and 14. The words 'is not' refer to the physical death of the beast, followed by his ascent from the abyss (17:8), which refers to his return to life (13:14) and is the same as his reappearance as the eighth king of 17:11."[28] "The twofold reference to the beast going to destruction or perdition (17:8,11) is the same as his eternal confinement in the lake of fire (19:20). The description of the beast in Revelation 17 likewise contains many similarities to the sword-wounded beast who was healed."[29] William Lee concludes: "The language is quite similar, the astonishment of the world's inhabitants identical, and the threefold emphasis on this spectacular feature is repeated in both contexts (13:3,12,14; 17:8,11)."[30]

Second Thessalonians 2:11-12 says, "For this reason God will send upon them a deluding influence so that they will believe what is false, in order that they all may be judged who did not believe the truth, but took pleasure in wickedness." God is the one who enables Satan and his disciples to do these things in a similar way in which He would use any human instrument to work genuine miracles. Harris tells us,

> The possibility of the beast's return to life (with either God's sovereign permission or His active working) should not be readily ruled out. In other words it is not impossible that the Antichrist should return to life because of the unique status of the Tribulation and the increased capacity of satanic power during that time, as well as God's broadening the parameters of what He will either permit or accomplish directly.[31]

For these reasons, I believe the Antichrist will die and come back to life. This will be part of the dramatic deception God will allow upon Earth during that special season of time.

APPENDIX B:

A Proposed Chronology of the End Times

In many of my books on end-times prophecy I like to include this outline at the end. I recognize it's not easy to try to fit together all the events of the end times into a chronological sequence. This outline is my best attempt, at this time, to put the pieces together. I certainly wouldn't insist on the correctness of every detail in this outline, but my prayer is that it will help you get a better grasp of the overall flow of events during the end times.

I. Events in Heaven

A. The Rapture of the Church (1 Corinthians 15:51-58; 1 Thessalonians 4:13-18; Revelation 3:10)

B. The Judgment Seat of Christ (Romans 14:10; 1 Corinthians 3:9-15; 4:1-5; 9:24-27; 2 Corinthians 5:10)

C. The Marriage of the Lamb (2 Corinthians 11:2; Revelation 19:6-8)

D. The Singing of Two Special Songs (Revelation 4–5)

E. The Lamb Receiving the Seven-Sealed Scroll (Revelation 5)

II. Events on Earth

A. The Seven-Year Tribulation

    1. Beginning of the Tribulation

        a. Seven-year Tribulation begins when the Antichrist signs a covenant with Israel, bringing peace to Israel and Jerusalem (Daniel 9:27; Ezekiel 38:8,11).

        b. The Jewish temple in Jerusalem is rebuilt (Daniel 9:27; Revelation 11:1).

        c. The reunited Roman Empire emerges in a ten-nation confederation (Daniel 2:40-44; 7:7; Revelation 17:12)

    2. First Half (3½ Years) of the Tribulation

        a. The seven seal judgments are opened (Revelation 6).

        b. The 144,000 Jewish believers begin their great evangelistic ministry (Revelation 7).

        c. Gog and his allies invade Israel, while Israel is at peace under the covenant with Antichrist, and are supernaturally decimated by God (Daniel 11:40-45; Ezekiel 38–39). This will probably occur somewhere near the end of the 3½-year period. The destruction of these forces will create a major shift in the balance of power that will enable the Antichrist to begin his rise to world ascendancy.

3. The Midpoint of the Tribulation

a. Antichrist breaks his covenant with Israel and invades the land (Daniel 9:27; 11:40-41).

b. Antichrist begins to consolidate his empire by plundering Egypt, Sudan, and Libya, whose armies have just been destroyed by God in Israel (Daniel 11:42-43; Ezekiel 38–39).

c. While in North Africa, Antichrist hears disturbing news of insurrection in Israel and immediately returns there to destroy and annihilate many (Daniel 11:44).

d. Antichrist sets up the abomination of desolation in the rebuilt temple in Jerusalem (Daniel 9:27; 11:45; Matthew 24:15; 2 Thessalonians 2:4; Revelation 13:5,15-18).

e. Sometime during these events the Antichrist is violently killed, possibly as a result of a war or an assassination (Daniel 11:45; Revelation 13:3,12,14; 17:8).

f. Satan is cast down from heaven and begins to make war with the woman, Israel (Revelation 12:7-13). The chief means he uses to persecute Israel is the two beasts in Revelation 13.

g. The faithful Jewish remnant flee to Petra in modern-day Jordan, where they are divinely protected for the remainder of the Tribulation (Matthew 24:16-20; Revelation 12:15-17).

h. The Antichrist is miraculously raised from the dead, to the awestruck amazement of the entire world (Revelation 13:3).

i. After his resurrection from the dead, the Antichrist gains political control over the ten kings of the reunited Roman Empire. Three of these kings will be killed by the Antichrist and the other seven will submit to him (Daniel 7:24; Revelation 17:12-13).

j. The two witnesses begin their 3½-year ministry (Revelation 11:2-3).

k. Antichrist and the ten kings destroy the religious system of Babylon and set up their religious capital in the city (Revelation 17:16-17).

4. Last Half (3½ years) of the Tribulation

a. Antichrist blasphemes God and the false prophet performs great signs and wonders and promotes false worship of the Antichrist (Revelation 13:5,11-15).

b. The mark of the beast (666) is introduced and enforced by the false prophet (Revelation 13:16-18).

c. Totally energized by Satan, the Antichrist dominates the world politically, religiously, and economically (Revelation 13:4-5,15-18).

d. The trumpet judgments are unleashed throughout the final half of the Tribulation (Revelation 8–9).

e. Knowing he has only a short time left, Satan intensifies his relentless, merciless persecution of the Jewish people and Gentile believers on earth (Daniel 7:25; Revelation 12:12; 13:15; 20:4).

5. The End of the Tribulation

   a. The bowl judgments are poured out in rapid succession (Revelation 16).

   b. The Campaign of Armageddon begins (Revelation 16:16).

   c. Commercial Babylon is destroyed (Revelation 18).

   d. The two witnesses are killed by Antichrist and are resurrected by God three-and-a-half days later (Revelation 11:7-12).

   e. Christ returns to the Mount of Olives and slays the armies gathered against Him throughout the land, from Megiddo to Petra (Revelation 19:11-16; see also Isaiah 34:1-6; 63:1-5).

   f. The birds gather to feed on the carnage (Revelation 19:17-18).

B. After the Tribulation

   1. Interval or Transition Period of 75 Days (Daniel 12:12)

      a. The Antichrist and the false prophet are cast into the lake of fire (Revelation 19:20-21).

      b. The abomination of desolation is removed from the temple (Daniel 12:11).

      c. Israel is regathered (Matthew 24:31).

      d. Israel is judged (Ezekiel 20:30-39; Matthew 25:1-30).

      e. Gentiles are judged (Matthew 25:31-46).

    f. Satan is bound in the abyss (Revelation 20:1-3).

    g. Old Testament and Tribulation saints are resurrected (Daniel 12:1-3; Isaiah 26:19; Revelation 20:4).

2. 1000-Year Reign of Christ on Earth (Revelation 20:4-6)

3. Satan's Final Revolt and Defeat (Revelation 20:7-10)

4. The Great White Throne Judgment of the Lost (Revelation 20:11-15)

5. The Destruction of the Present Heavens and Earth (Matthew 24:35; 2 Peter 3:3-12; Revelation 21:1)

6. The Creation of the New Heavens and New Earth (Isaiah 65:17; 66:22; 2 Peter 3:13; Revelation 21:1)

7. Eternity (Revelation 21:9–22:5)

NOTES

Chapter 1—Financial Apocalypse Brings an Economic New World Order

1. "600K jobs lost in January," *The Daily Oklahoman* (February 7, 2009), 1B.

2. Robert J. Samuelson, "The Stunted Economic Stimulus," *Newsweek* (March 2, 2009), 28.

3. "Another Inconvenient Truth," *The Economist* (August 16, 2008), 68.

4. Jon Meacham and Evan Thomas, "We Are All Socialists Now," *Newsweek* (February 16, 2009), 23-24.

5. I heard this statistic on "Your World," Fox News (February 17, 2009).

6. "UKs Brown: Now is the time to build global society," Reuters.com (November 9, 2008).

7. Frank Millar, "Brown to discuss 'global new deal' with Obama," Irishtimes.com (March 1, 2009).

8. Jim Puzzanghera and Maura Reynolds, "Pressure builds for a global economic strategy," *Los Angeles Times,* (October 10, 2008), at www.articles.latimes.com/2008/Oct/10/business/fi-global10.

9. Robert Reich, *The Work of Nations* (New York: Alfred Knopf, 1992), 3.

10. David R. Sands, "Financial crisis reshapes world order," *Washington Times* (October 12, 2008).

11. Christine Harper, "There is going to be a new financial world order that will be born of this," *Bloomberg* (September 16, 2008).

12. "Global financial crisis: does the world need a new banking 'policeman'?" *The Telegraph* (October 8, 2008).

13. Drew Zahn, "Kissinger: Obama primed to create 'New World Order': Policy guru says global upheaval presents great opportunity'" *WorldNetDaily* (January 6, 2009) www.worldnetdaily.com/index.php/index.php?pageId=85442.

14. contenderministries.org/UN/globalismquotes.php.

15. Zahn, "Kissinger: Obama primed to create 'New World Order.'"

16. Zahn, "Kissinger: Obama primed to create 'New World Order.'"

17. Jerome R. Corsis, "Kissinger affirms call for 'new world order' Proposes globalism to solve current world economic crisis," *WorldNetDaily* (January 15, 2009), www.wnd.com/index.php?fa=PAGE.view&pageId=86229.

18. Simon Hooper, "Davos delegates gather to shape 'new world,'" CNN.com (January 27, 2009), www.edition.cnn.com/2009/BUSINESS/01/27/davos.tuesday.crisis/index.html.

19. Justin Fox, "New World Order," *Time* (February 16, 2009), 29.

20. "China urges new currency order after 'financial tsunami,'" Reuters.com (September 17, 2008).

21. Tim LaHaye and Jerry B. Jenkins, *Are We Living in the Last Days?* (Wheaton, IL: Tyndale House, 1999), 203.

22. Phillip Goodman, "The Economy At the End Time," *The Spirit of Prophecy* (September-October 2008).

Chapter 2—The Future Has Already Been Written

1. I say 19 judgments instead of 21 because the seventh seal contains the seven bowls, and apparently the seventh trumpet contains the seven bowls.

Chapter 3—Your Future Is in the Cards

1. "Visa the Credit Card of Real Men," Pretzel Logic (December 3, 2007), www.borntorun1647.blogspot.com/2007/12/visa-credit-card-of-real-man.html.

2. Judy Warner, "Visa Takes on Cash for First Time," *Media Post* (November 17, 2006), www.publications.mediapost.com/index.cfm?fuseaction=Articles.show/Article&art_aid=51276&art_type=16.

3. Robert J. Samuelson, "The Vanishing Greenback," *Newsweek* (June 20, 2007), www.newsweek.com/id/33697.

4. Robert J. Samuelson, "The Vanishing Greenback."

5. The headlines are from the following five articles:

   • www.corporate.visa.com/md/nr/press724.jsp

   • findarticles.com/p/articles/mi_m0EIN/is_1995_May_31/ai_16931997/

   • www.allbusiness.com/consumer-products/food-beverage-products-nonalcoholics/10555566-1.html

   • www.usatech.com/company_info/news/usa_2006_07_10.php

   • findarticles.com/p/articles/mi_m0EIN/is_2007_July_2/ai_n19330388

6. Daniel Stone, "The Greener Way to Pay," *Newsweek* (December 1, 2008), 50.

7. "Out of financial chaos, futurist predicts cashless society and robocops" (September 22, 2008), www.aftermathnews.wordpress.com/2008/09/22/out-of-financial-chaos-futurist-predicts-cashless-society-and-robocops/.

8. Liz Moyer, "The Myth of the Cashless Society" (February 14, 2006), www.forbes.com/2006/02/11/cashless-society-cash_cx_em_money06_0214cashless.html.

9. "Walmart lowers cost of its money cards," Associated Press, February 18, 2009.

10. All of these inventions were cited by Tom Wilmes, "The Future of Shopping," *Spirit* (April 2008), 98-105.

11. Wilmes, "The Future of Shopping."

12. Jose Fermosa, "McDonald's Tries Out New RFID-Enabled Pay-By-Phone Coupons," (February 16, 2009), www.justgetthere.us/blog/plugin/tag/cashless+society.

13. Wilmes, "The Future of Shopping."

14. Wilmes, "The Future of Shopping."

15. Cited from www.ssa.gov/deposit/DDFAQ898.htm.

16. "Americans rank direct deposit their top financial management tool" (February 6, 2008), www.fms.treas.gov/news/press/go_direct_month.htm.

17. Cited from www.smartcardalliance.org/pages/smart-car.

18. Maria Bruno-Britz, "Is the End of Cash at Hand?" Bank Systems & Technology (September 28, 2005), www.banktech.com/story/showArticle.jhtml?articleID=171201571.

19. Cited from www.smartcardalliance.org/pages/smart-car.

20. Joseph Schuler, "A cash-free society: nirvana or nightmare?" at www.thefreelibrary.com/A+cash-free+society:+nirvana+or+nightmare%3F-a014713842.

21. Thomas Ice and Timothy Demy, *The Coming Cashless Society* (Eugene, OR: Harvest House, 1996), 25.

22. Ice and Demy, *The Coming Cashless Society*, 36.

23. Terry L. Cook, *The Mark of the New World Order* (Springdale, PA: Whitaker House, 1996), 203-04.

Chapter 4—The Coming Cashless Society

1. Edward Bellamy, *Looking Backward: From 2000 to 1887* (Boston: Houghton, Mifflin, 1888; reprint, Bedford, MA: Applewood Books, 2000), 55, 148, 204.

2. Bellamy, *Looking Backward: From 2000 to 1887,* 56.

3. "American to Move to Cashless Cabins," *The New York Times* (February 22, 2009).

4. "United cabins go cashless within North America, USA Today (February 27, 2009), www.usatoday.com/travel/flights/2009-02-27-united-cashless_N.htm.

5. "Monopoly Ditches Cash," at www.dvice.com/archives/2006/07/monopoly_ditches_cash_ruins_ch.php.

6. Darren Murph, "Monopoly Ditches Cash, Goes Plastic" (July 24, 2006), www.engadget.com/2006/07/24/monopoly-ditches-cash-goes-plastic/.

7. Cited from www.rfidjournal.com/.

8. Cited from www.aimglobal.org/technologies/rfid/.

9. "Sky Tek Enables Cashless Payment at Cold-Drink Vending Machines at Atlanta International Airport," *Business Wire,* April 2, 2007.

10. *The Economist* (May 3, 2001).

11. *USA Today* (December 9, 2008), 9C.

12. Cited from www.done-with-irs.com/2009/01/20/cashless-society-2/.

13. Tim LaHaye and Jerry B. Jenkins, *Are We Living in the Last Days?* (Wheaton, IL: Tyndale House, 1999), 201.

14. LaHaye and Jenkins, *Are We Living in the Last Days?*

15. Rebecca Camber, "Barclaycard unveils plans for paying using your mobile phone, key fob or fingerprints," MailOnline (September 9, 2008).

16. "The Future of Money," *The Economist* (February 15, 2007), www.economist.com/finance/displaystory.cfm?story_id=8697424.

17. Hal Lindsey, *The Late Great Planet Earth* (Grand Rapids: Zondervan, 1970), 113.

Chapter 5—Biometrics and the Beast

1. This list comes from "The Cashless Society: Buddy Can You Spare Me a Card-Swipe," (March 7, 2007), www.pinkslipblog.blogspot.com/2007/03/cashless-society-buddy-can-you-spare-me.html.

2. Jaikumar Vijayan, "Calif. DMV tried to sneak in biometrics for driver's licenses, groups claim," *Computer World* (February 5, 2009).

3. Sherrie Gossett, "Bio-chip implant arrives for cashless transactions," www.WorldNetDaily.com (November 21, 2003).

4. Chris Maxcer, "U.S. to Enlist 20-Petaflop Supercomputer for Nuke Management Duty," *TechNewsWorld* (February 3, 2009), at www.technewsworld.com/story/66067.html.

5. Cited from www.culturevulture.net/Movies/MinorityReport.htm.

6. Tim LaHaye and Jerry B. Jenkins, *Are We Living in the Last Days?* (Wheaton, IL: Tyndale House, 1999), 198-99.

7. LaHaye and Jenkins, *Are We Living in the Last Days?*, 199 (emphasis added).

Chapter 6—Rise of the G-10

1. Leon Wood, *A Commentary on Daniel* (Grand Rapids: Zondervan, 1973), 71.
2. Randall Price, *Jerusalem in Prophecy: God's Stage for the Final Drama* (Eugene, OR: Harvest House, 1998), 50.

Chapter 7—Runaway Inflation Rocks the World

1. "The German Hyperinflation, 1923" at www.pbs.org/wgbh/commandingheights/shared/minitext/ess_germanhyperinflation.html.
2. Sebastien Berger, "Zimbabwe hyperinflation will set world record within six weeks," *The Telegraph* (November 13, 2008) www.telegraph.co.uk/news/worldnews/.../zimbabwe/3453540/Zimbabwe-hyperinflation-will-set-world-record-within-six-weeks.html.
3. "Hyperinflation forces Zimbabwe to print $200 million notes," (December 7, 2008), www.cnn.com/2008/WORLD/africa/12/06/zimbabwe.currency/index.html.
4. Billy Graham, *Approaching Hoofbeats* (Waco, TX: Word Books, 1983), 161.
5. Robert L. Thomas, *Revelation 1–7: An Exegetical Commentary* (Chicago: Moody, 1992), 430.
6. John F. Walvoord, *The Revelation of Jesus Christ* (Chicago: Moody, 1966), 129.
7. Henry M. Morris, *The Revelation Record* (Wheaton, IL: Tyndale House, 1983), 116.

Chapter 8—One World Under Antichrist

1. "Bible Prophecy Basics: The Rise of Antichrist" at www.angelfire.com/realm/ofstardust/RISE_AC.html.
2. Paul Johnson, "A World in Search of Leaders," *Forbes* (November 24, 2008), 29.
3. H.L. Willmington, *The King Is Coming* (Wheaton, IL: Tyndale House, 1981), 81.
4. Arthur W. Pink, *The Antichrist* (Grand Rapids: Kregel, 1988), 9.
5. Pink, *The Antichrist*, 81.
6. Willmington, *The King Is Coming*, 95.
7. Willmington, *The King Is Coming*, 66-67.
8. The verb "is coming" in 1 John 2:18 is a futuristic present, which "assumes the future coming of the antichrist to be as certain as the present reality." D. Edmond Hiebert, *The Epistles of John* (Greenville, SC: Bob Jones University Press, 1991), 109.
9. Here is a small sample of the scholars who believe 1 John speaks of a future personal Antichrist: F.F. Bruce, *The Epistles of John* (Grand Rapids: Eerdmans, 1992), 64-68;

Martyn Lloyd-Jones, *Walking with God: Life in Christ* (Wheaton, IL: Crossway, 1993), 98-101; R.C.H. Lenski, *The Interpretation of the Epistles of St. Peter, St. John and St. Jude* (Minneapolis: Augsburg, 1966), 430-32; James Montgomery Boice, *The Epistles of John* (Grand Rapids: Zondervan, 1979), 84-86; Simon J. Kistemaker, *James and I—III John,* New Testament Commentary (Grand Rapids: Baker, 1986), 275-76; I. Howard Marshall, *The Epistles of John,* The New International Commentary on the New Testament, gen. ed. F.F. Bruce (Grand Rapids: Eerdmans, 1978), 148-51; John R.W. Stott, *The Letters of John,* Tyndale New Testament Commentaries (Grand Rapids: Eerdmans, 1994), 108-10; D. Edmond Hiebert, *The Epistles of John,* 106-09. The only respected evangelical scholar I could find who did not hold that 1 John 2:18 refers to the coming of a future personal Antichrist was Brooke Foss Westcott. And Westcott was not decisive. All he said was that the passage is "not decisive as to St. John's teaching in regard to the coming of one great Antichrist, of which the others were preparatory embodiments." B.F. Westcott, *The Epistles of John* (Grand Rapids: Eerdmans, 1966), 70. Bernard McGinn, who is not an evangelical Christian, but wrote a masterpiece on the subject of Antichrist, says that the use of the singular for antichrist in 1 John, "made it possible for most later Christians to believe in many antichrists as well as in the single final opposer predicted in 2 Thessalonians and the Apocalypse." Bernard McGinn, *Antichrist: Two Thousand Years of the Human Fascination with Evil* (San Francisco: Harper, 1994), 56.

10. James Montgomery Boice, *The Epistles of John: An Expositional Commentary* (Grand Rapids: Zondervan Publishing, 1979), 86.

11. F.F. Bruce, *The Epistles of John* (Grand Rapids: Eerdmans, 1992), 65.

12. Grant R. Jeffrey, *Prince of Darkness* (Toronto: Frontier Research, 1994), 29.

13. Jeffrey, *Prince of Darkness,* 30.

14. J. Dwight Pentecost, *Will Man Survive?* (Grand Rapids: Zondervan, 1971), 93.

15. Joel Richardson, *Antichrist: Islam's Awaited Messiah* (Enumclaw, WA: Pleasant Word, 2006), 52-70.

16. Kenneth L. Woodward, "What the Bible Says About the End of the World," *Newsweek* (November 1, 1999), 69.

17. Gary Frazier, *Signs of the Coming of Christ* (Arlington, TX: Discovery Ministries, 1998), 149.

Chapter 9—The Coming World Commerce Secretary

1. John Phillips, *Exploring Revelation* (Neptune, NJ: Loizeaux Brothers, 1991), 171.

Chapter 10—Babylon, the Great City

1. Billy Graham, *World Aflame* (Old Tappan, NJ: Fleming Revell, 1965), 193.

2. Henry Morris, *The Revelation Record* (Wheaton, IL: Tyndale House, 1983), 323.

3. Charles Dyer, *The Rise of Babylon* (Wheaton, IL: Tyndale House, 1991), 182.

4. Robert Thomas, *Revelation 8–22* (Chicago: Moody, 1995), 307.

5. Morris, *The Revelation Record*, 348-49.

6. Charles H. Dyer, "The Identity of Babylon in Revelation 17-18," *Bibliotheca Sacra* 144 (October-December 1987): 441-43.

7. Khalid al-Ansary, "Babylon's Future Written in Its Ruins" (February 11, 2009, at www.reuters.com/article/middleeastcrisis/idUSL9399801.

8. Khalid al-Ansary, "Babylon's Future."

9. Jad Mouawad, "Construction Site Called Saudi Arabia," *The New York Times* (January 20, 2008), www.nytimes.com/2008/01/20/business/worldbusiness/20saudi.html.

10. Bobby Ghosh, "A New City in the Saudi Desert," *Time* (October 2, 2008), www.time.com/time/world/article/0,8599,1846200,00.html.

Chapter 11—Unlocking the Mystery of the Mark—666

1. Gary DeMar, *End Times Fiction* (Nashville, TN: Thomas Nelson, 2001), 142-45; Kenneth Gentry, *The Beast of Revelation* (Tyler, TX: Institute for Christian Economics, 1989).

2. Gentry, *The Beast of Revelation*, 35. O. Ruhle says that the 616 variant was an attempt to link Gaius Caesar (Caligula) to the beast out of the sea in Revelation 13. The numerical value of his name in Greek equals 616. Gerhard Kittel, ed. *The Theological Dictionary of the New Testament*, trans. Geoffrey W. Bromiley, vol. 1 (Grand Rapids: Eerdmans, 1964), 462-63.

3. Gentry, *The Beast of Revelation*, 53-54.

4. For a thorough discussion of the date of Revelation, see Mark Hitchcock, "The Stake in the Heart: The A.D. 95 Date of Revelation" in *The End Times Controversy* (Eugene, OR: Harvest House, 2003), 123-50.

5. Robert L. Thomas, *Revelation 8–22: An Exegetical Commentary* (Chicago: Moody, 1995), 179-80.

6. David E. Aune, *Revelation 6–16*, Word Biblical Commentary, gen. ed. Bruce M. Metzger, vol. 52B (Nashville, TN: Thomas Nelson, 1998), 771.

7. For a complete refutation of the view that Nero is the beast of Revelation 13, see, Andy Woods, "Revelation 13 and the First Beast" in *The End Times Controversy* (Eugene, OR: Harvest House, 2003), 237-50.

8. Irenaeus, who wrote in the late second century, suggested three names for the total 666: Evanthas, Lateinos, and Teitan (*Against Heresies* 5.30.3). But he never suggested Nero.

9. Simon J. Kistemaker, *Exposition of the Book of Revelation*, New Testament Commentary (Grand Rapids: Baker, 2001), 395.

10. Thomas, *Revelation 8–22*, 185.

11. William F. Arndt and F. W. Gingrich, *A Greek-English Lexicon of the New Testament* (Chicago: University of Chicago Press, 1957), 876.

12. Thomas, *Revelation 8–22*, 181.

13. Henry Morris, *Revelation Record* (Wheaton, IL: Tyndale House, 1983), 252.

14. Hal Harless, "666: The Beast and His Mark in Revelation 13," *The Conservative Theological Journal* (December 2003): 342-46.

15. Henry Morris, *Revelation Record* (Wheaton, IL: Tyndale House, 1983), 255.

16. Arnold G. Fruchtenbaum, *The Footsteps of the Messiah,* rev. ed. (Tustin, CA: Ariel Publications, 2003), 255.

17. Fruchtenbaum, *The Footsteps of the Messiah,* 255.

18. John F. Walvoord. *The Prophecy Knowledge Handbook* (Wheaton, IL: SP Publications, 1990), 587.

19. M.R. DeHaan, *Studies in Revelation* (Grand Rapids: Zondervan, 1946; reprint, Grand Rapids: Kregel, 1998), 189.

20. Morris, *Revelation Record,* 256.

21. Morris, *Revelation Record.*

22. The word used for the seal of God on the foreheads of the saints in Revelation 7:3 is the Greek word *sphragizo,* which is used of the invisible seal of the Holy Spirit in the New Testament (2 Corinthians 1:22; Ephesians 1:13; 4:30). The word "mark" (*charagma*), on the other hand, refers to a visible mark, imprint, or etching. Therefore, while God's mark on His saints will be invisible, the beast's mark will be visible.

23. John F. Walvoord, *Prophecy: 14 Essential Keys to Understanding the Final Drama* (Nashville, TN: Thomas Nelson Publishers, 1993), 125.

24. Steven Levy, "Playing the ID Card," *Newsweek* (May 13, 2002), 44-46.

Chapter 13—Cashless and You

1. Thomas Ice and Timothy Demy, *The Coming Cashless Society* (Eugene, OR: Harvest House, 1996), 168.

2. Ice and Demy, *The Coming Cashless Society,* 169-70.

Some Questions You Might Be Asking

1. Gary DeMar, *End Times Fiction* (Nashville, TN: Thomas Nelson, 2001), 134-37.

2. *Didache* 16.4. Gary DeMar maintains that the false messiahs in Mark 13:22 were present in the days before the destruction of the temple in A.D. 70 and that Nero

was the beast of Revelation 13. But the *Didache,* which was written after A.D. 70, refers to a future individual who will fulfill these prophecies.

3. Irenaeus, *Against Heresies* 5.28.2.

4. Irenaeus, *Against Heresies* 5.30.2.

5. Irenaeus, *Against Heresies* 5.25.3-4.

6. Hippolytus, *Antichrist* 6. Cf. Bernard McGinn, *Antichrist* (San Francisco: Harper, 1994), 61.

7. Bernard McGinn, *Antichrist: Two Thousand Years of the Human Fascination with Evil* (San Francisco: Harper, 1994), 61.

8. McGinn, *Antichrist,* 63.

9. Cyril, *Catechetical Lectures* 15.12-15.

10. Jerome, *Commentary on Daniel* 7:8; 11:39; 11:45. Unlike most of the other early writers, Jerome did not support the view that the Antichrist would rebuild the temple in Jerusalem. He also strongly rejected any idea of a literal 1000-year reign of Christ. But he did believe in a future, personal Antichrist. Jerome believed that Daniel 7–11, 2 Thessalonians 2, Matthew 24, Revelation 17, and John 5:43 all related to the future Antichrist. John Chrysostom also rejected the idea of a rebuilt temple, but he too believed in a personal Antichrist in the end times. *Homily 3 on 2 Thess.*

11. McGinn, *Antichrist,* 63.

12. McGinn, *Antichrist,* 78.

13. There are at least 11 different views on the identity of the restrainer in 2 Thessalonians 2: 1) the Roman Empire, 2) the Jewish state, 3) the apostle Paul, 4) the preaching of the gospel, 5) human government, 6) Satan, 7) Elijah, 8) some unknown heavenly being, 9) Michael the archangel, 10) the Holy Spirit, and 11) the church.

14. Donald Grey Barnhouse, *Thessalonians: An Expositional Commentary* (Grand Rapids: Zondervan, 1977), 99-100.

15. Hank Hanegraaff, *The Apocalypse Code: Find Out What the Bible Really Says About the End Times and Why It Matters Today* (Nashville, TN: Thomas Nelson, 2007), xix–xx.

16. Hank Hanegraaff and Sigmund Brouwer, *The Last Disciple* (Wheaton, IL: Tyndale House, 2004), 394.

17. William F. Arndt and F.W. Gingrich, *A Greek-English Lexicon of the New Testament* (Chicago: University of Chicago Press, 1957), 55.

18. George Abbott-Smith, *A Manual Greek Lexicon of the New Testament,* 3d ed. (Edinburgh: T & T Clark, 1937), 443.

19. Joseph Henry Thayer, *A Greek-English Lexicon of the New Testament* (New York: American Book Company, 1889), 620.

20. Gregory H. Harris, "Satan's Deceptive Miracles in the Tribulation," *Bibliotheca Sacra* 156 (July-September 1999): 310.

21. Harris, "Satan's Deceptive Miracles in the Tribulation."

22. Philip Edgcumbe Hughes, *A Commentary on the Epistle to the Hebrews* (Grand Rapids: Eerdmans, 1977), 80-81.

23. Harris, "Satan's Deceptive Miracles in the Tribulation," 311.

24. Harris, "Satan's Deceptive Miracles in the Tribulation."

25. Harris, "Satan's Deceptive Miracles in the Tribulation."

26. Charles C. Ryrie, *Revelation,* Everyman's Bible Commentary (Chicago: Moody, 1968), 83.

27. Gregory H. Harris, "The Wound of the Beast in the Tribulation," *Bibliotheca Sacra* 156 (October-December 1999): 467.

28. Harris, "The Wound of the Beast in the Tribulation."

29. Harris, "The Wound of the Beast in the Tribulation."

30. William Lee, "The Revelation of St. John" in *The Holy Bible,* vol. 4 (London: John Murray, 1881), 89.

31. Harris, "The Wound of the Beast in the Tribulation," 469.

Available October 2009

In *2012, the Bible, and the End of the World*, Mark Hitchcock explores a fascinating last-days controversy that is gaining the attention of millions all over the globe.

What should Christians make of the rapidly spreading speculations that the world will end on December 21, 2012? The ancient Mayans were expert astronomers and their advanced calendar cycles predict 12/21/2012 as a catastrophic day of apocalypse. This prophecy has spawned a growing number of fringe-element books, Web sites, and even a major movie complete with an all-star cast.

Missing in the furor is a biblical perspective. In this book, Hitchcock examines the following questions:

- Why December 21, 2012?
- Can we trust the Mayan alarm clock?
- Does the Bible say anything about 2012?
- What signs will tell us that Armageddon is near?

A fascinating survey of both the historical past and the prophetic future.

OTHER BIBLE PROPHECY BOOKS
BY HARVEST HOUSE PUBLISHERS

Charting the End Times
Tim LaHaye and Thomas Ice

The result of decades of research and Bible study, this landmark resource provides a fascinating picture of the end times. Includes visual foldouts, explanatory text, 50 color charts/diagrams, and clear answers to tough questions.

Charting the End Times CD
Tim LaHaye and Thomas Ice

Includes all the charts from the book, a Windows/Macintosh CD-ROM. Both Windows and Macintosh compatible.

The Popular Encyclopedia of Bible Prophecy
Tim LaHaye and Ed Hindson, general editors

An A-to-Z encyclopedia filled with over 400 pages of facts, information, and charts about the last days.

The Popular Bible Prophecy Commentary
Tim LaHaye and Ed Hindson, general editors

It's all here—clear and concise explanations for key prophetic passages from Genesis to Revelation. Written by Bible scholars but created for lay-level Bible students, this includes useful charts, diagrams, and time lines that enhance one's understanding of Bible prophecy.